Mastering Angular Signals:

A Practical Guide to Modern Reactivity, Performance, and Migration

Muhammad Ahsan Ayaz
GDE in Angular, Speaker, Software Architect

About the Author

Muhammad Ahsan Ayaz is a father, a son, a brother to two awesome siblings, a husband to a caring and supportive wife, a Muslim, a Google Developer Expert (GDE) in Angular, an experienced Software Architect, and an active speaker within the international tech community. With a deep passion for modern web development, Ahsan focuses on building performant, scalable, and maintainable applications, keenly following and implementing the latest advancements in frameworks like Angular.

He is also the author of the "Angular Cookbook" (ng-cookbook.com), where he previously shared practical solutions and patterns for common challenges faced by Angular developers.

He has also developed multiple open-sourced libraries and tools, including the ***ngx-device-detector*** library which helps identify the device, operating system, etc that your Angular app is running on. This library alone is used by over ***5,000*** projects on GitHub, with over ***12 million*** installs.

Ahsan runs a community called “Code with Ahsan” with over 25000 subscribers on YouTube, 20000 on Facebook, 64000 on Instagram, and over 1600 members subscribing to his “AHSYNC BYTES” newsletter (blog.codewithahsan.dev). He loves mentoring, discussing tech, AI, and tools for developers productivity, and to create tech content on social platforms.

Ahsan's extensive experience with Angular's evolution, combined with his active engagement with the developer community and insights into their questions surrounding reactivity, inspired him to write "Mastering Angular Signals." His goal with this book is to provide a comprehensive, practical guide that empowers developers to confidently leverage Angular Signals for building the next generation of sophisticated and efficient web applications.

About the Reviewer

Sonu Kapoor is a Google Developer Expert (GDE) in Angular and a Microsoft Most Valuable Professional (MVP) with a career spanning over 20 years in web development. A trusted Angular Collaborator and core contributor to community-driven features like Typed Forms, Sonu is widely recognized for his architectural expertise and deep insights into scalable frontend development.

He is the author of AI-Powered App Development: Leveraging AI for Practical Solutions and Beginning JavaScript Syntax, both of which reflect his commitment to empowering developers with modern, practical knowledge.

As the technical editor of Master Angular Signals, Sonu ensured the book's technical rigor, real-world relevance, and clarity, making it a reliable guide for developers at all levels.

About the Code Examples

This book takes a practical, hands-on approach to mastering **Angular Signals**. To complement the explanations and concepts discussed, a dedicated code repository containing runnable examples for each chapter is available on GitHub.

Repository: github.com/AhsanAyaz/mastering-angular-signals-book

I strongly encourage you to clone this repository, explore the code, and run the examples as you progress through the book. Experimenting with the code is one of the best ways to solidify your understanding.

Structure:

The repository is structured to mirror the book's chapters. You will find the components and services discussed within the src/app/components/ directory, organized by chapter number (e.g., `apps/chapter-02/`, `apps/chapter-03/`, etc.). Specific examples within chapters often reside in subdirectories named after the concept being illustrated (e.g., `signal`, `effect`, `linkedSignal`).

Running the Examples:

Clone the repository:

```
git clone
https://github.com/AhsanAyaz/mastering-angular-signals-book.git
cd mastering-angular-signals-book
```

Install dependencies:

First, ensure you have Node.js and npm (or yarn/pnpm) installed. Then, install the project dependencies and the Nx CLI globally:

```
# install project dependencies
npm install
```

```
# install nx globally
```

```
npm add --global nx@latest
```

Why Nx? Nx helps us manage the various chapter examples within this single code repository (a 'monorepo'). It simplifies running specific examples (like `nx serve chapter-01`) and allows us to easily share common code, like UI components, between different chapters, keeping things organized and efficient.

Serve an app:

To run the examples for a specific chapter, use the `nx serve` command followed by the chapter's application name (usually chapter-XX):

```
nx serve chapter-01
```

This will typically launch the application in your browser at *http://localhost:4200/*. The application includes a navigation menu corresponding to the chapter's code examples, allowing you to easily view each example in action.

Throughout the book, I will provide pointers to the specific directories relevant to the section you are reading. Happy experimenting!

Foreword

Angular has been a robust dependable framework in the development world since it launched in September 2016. Since then, the framework has been an innovator, moving the web development world forward with industry leading features while learning lessons and growing with the Angular developer community. Managing state and data is critical for applications large and small. Angular developers needed a solution that matched the quality of other foundation strengths provided by the framework. The Angular team is confident the solution is Angular Signals - the new reactivity API for simplifying and super-charging data and state management.

Now, as a reader, you have the incredible opportunity to learn about this new breakthrough in Angular application development from an industry expert and leader. Ahsan is a seasoned educator who has been helping developers learn about technology at the highest levels for years. With his new book he's bringing his wealth of experience and educator skills to Angular Signals for all to benefit from.

This book goes beyond introducing Signals with trivial examples. It provides deep insight and practical knowledge informed by years of experience building applications at enterprise levels. Reading this book positions you to exceed basic familiarity and sets you up for success in truly mastering Angular Signals.

Mark Thompson,

Developer Advocate, Team Angular @ Google

Preface

The world of web development is in constant flux, and Angular, as a leading framework, is no exception. Over the years, I've had the privilege of working with Angular, speaking about it, contributing to the community as a Google Developer Expert (GDE), and even distilling practical knowledge into works like the Angular Cookbook (*https://ng-cookbook.com*). Throughout this journey, one theme remains constant: the pursuit of building more efficient, maintainable, and reactive applications.

The introduction of ***Angular Signals*** marks one of the most significant evolutionary steps in the framework's history. It's not merely a new set of APIs; it represents a fundamental shift. A shift towards a more granular, explicit, and potentially much more performant way of managing state and reactivity, by eliminating dependency on RxJS for Angular's core reactivity paradigm. Seeing the excitement, the questions, and the need for a consolidated resource within the community spurred the creation of this book.

Modern Angular: Mastering Angular Signals is designed to be your comprehensive guide through this new landscape. Whether you're an experienced Angular developer looking to understand how Signals change the game, seeking to migrate existing RxJS-heavy applications, or starting fresh and wanting to leverage the latest and greatest from day one, this book is for you.

Building upon the practical, hands-on philosophy of the Angular Cookbook, we will journey together from the core concepts of **`signal()`**, **`computed()`**, and **`effect()`** to advanced topics like asynchronous operations with **`resource()`**, seamless component integration using the new **`input()`**, **`output()`**, and **`model()`** APIs, robust testing strategies, and effective migration techniques. We'll explore not just the 'how' but also the 'why,' delving into performance implications and architectural best practices.

My goal is to equip you not just with the knowledge but with the confidence to wield Signals effectively, enabling you to build the next generation of sophisticated, responsive, and efficient Angular applications. The future of Angular is increasingly signal-driven, and I'm excited to explore it with you.

Let's begin!

Muhammad Ahsan Ayaz

GDE in Angular, Speaker, Software Architect, Author of Angular Cookbook

Table of Contents

Chapter 1: Angular's Reactive Landscape

Introduction

In the ever-evolving world of Angular, a new era of reactivity has dawned. Angular Signals represent a paradigm shift, offering a more performant, simpler, and more predictable approach to building dynamic applications. **Angular**, one of the most popular frameworks for crafting modern web applications, is continuously being improved and this new reactivity model, **Signals**, is a vital new addition to the toolkit of every Angular developer.

Mastering Angular Signals is no longer optional; it's a crucial skill for any Angular developer aiming to stay current and build high-performance applications. With Signals, you can now write applications that react instantly to user actions and data changes, offering a smoother and more responsive user experience. This new model not only enhances performance but also reduces complexity, making your applications more maintainable and easier to reason about.

This book will guide you through mastering Angular Signals, from the fundamentals to advanced components/applications. We will take you on a journey, starting with core concepts, and will equip you to implement Signals in a variety of complex application scenarios, covering key topics such as `signal()`, `computed()`, `effect()`, `resource()`, `linkedSignal()` and more. We will also discuss the new component input/output syntax with `input()`, `model()`, and `output()`, which can all leverage the capabilities of Angular Signals.

By the end of this book, you will not only have a deep understanding of the Angular Signals, but you will also possess the ability to write more performant and efficient Angular applications. Moreover, you will master the new APIs introduced with Signals and gain the confidence to migrate your existing applications to a signal-based architecture. We will be focusing on a practical, hands-on approach, with real-world code examples and application scenarios.

This book is structured so that each chapter builds upon the previous one. We encourage you to try the code examples and experiment, as this will help you master the concepts quickly. We will explain all the code examples thoroughly and will make use of diagrams and illustrations as required. We will make sure that you have the necessary skills and understanding, and will provide all the necessary knowledge to succeed in the Angular ecosystem.

The future of Angular is still reactive, but without the need to maintain manual subscriptions, working with RxJS streams, and instead having a more fine-grained reactivity. And ***Signals*** are at the heart of it all. Let's embark on this journey together and unlock the full potential of modern Angular development!

The Need for Reactivity

In the world of modern web applications, users expect immediate feedback and dynamic updates to the user interface. When a user interacts with an application – for example, by clicking a button, updating a form, or browsing through data – the application must react promptly, updating the user interface and reflecting the changes. This interactivity and responsiveness are made possible by reactivity.

Reactivity is the ability of an application to automatically update its user interface whenever there are changes in its underlying data. In essence, when a piece of data changes, the user interface should update to reflect that change.

Before the introduction of Angular Signals, Angular primarily relied on two main mechanisms for managing reactivity: ***Zone.js*** and ***RxJS Observables***. While these mechanisms served their purpose, they also came with limitations and pain points.

- **Zone.js:** Angular utilizes Zone.js, a powerful library that patches asynchronous APIs (like `setTimeout`, `fetch` and event listeners) to trigger Angular's change detection mechanism. When asynchronous tasks complete, Zone.js notifies Angular, which then checks the component tree for any changes that need to be reflected on the UI. However, this can be quite inefficient as it can lead to unnecessary and frequent updates, especially in complex applications. For instance, imagine a single event triggering a full change detection cycle across the entire component tree, even if most components have no new data to render. This can cause significant performance issues, especially on lower-powered devices or with complex components, resulting in unnecessary re-renders, and thus a lagging user experience.

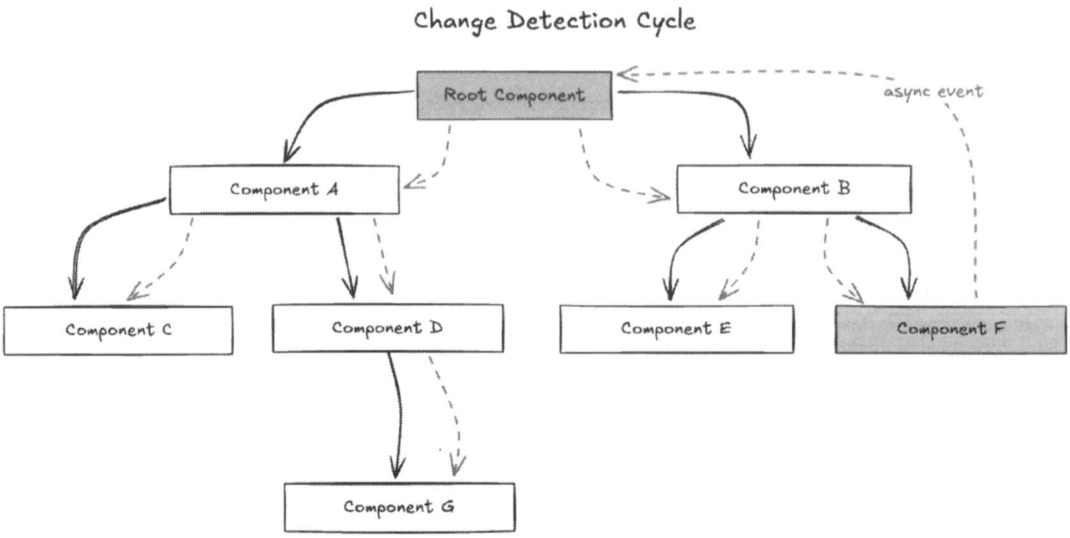

Figure 1.1 - Event in *Component F* triggers change detection cycle across the component tree

- **RxJS Observables:** While observables provided a way to manage asynchronous data streams, they also introduced some complexity, particularly when dealing with simple reactivity scenarios. While RxJS is invaluable for handling complex asynchronous operations, it was often seen as overkill for basic state updates and UI changes. It requires developers to subscribe and unsubscribe from streams, and often more code is needed to handle the lifecycle of observables.

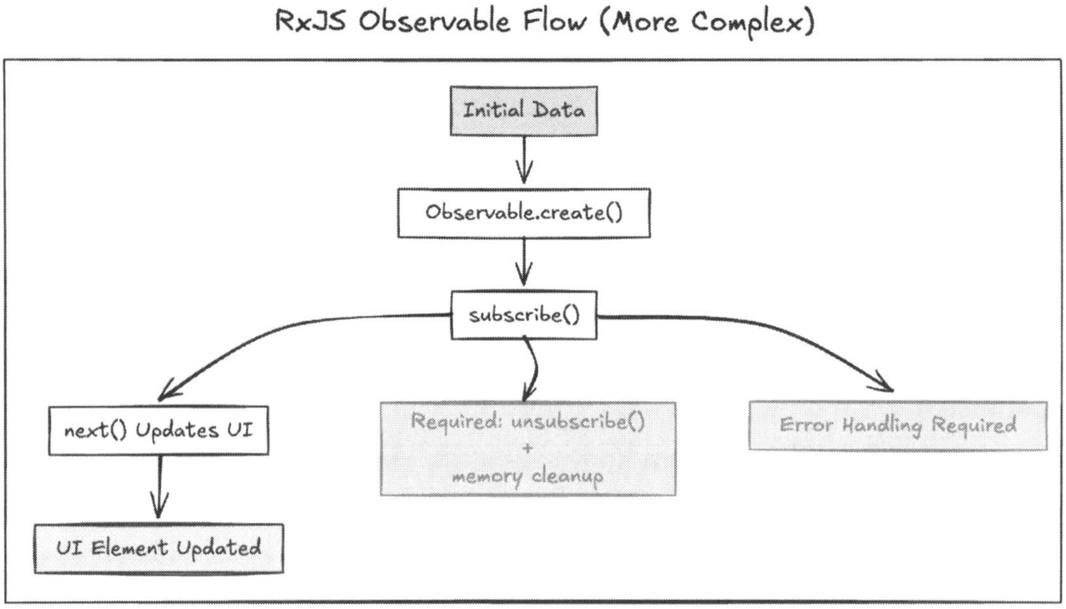

Figure 1.2 - RXJS Observables and required considerations

Introducing Angular Signals

Angular Signals are a new reactivity model introduced to address the shortcomings of previous methods. They provide a more efficient, simpler, and predictable way to manage state and propagate changes throughout your Angular applications. Unlike Zone.js, which triggers a full change detection cycle, Signals enable fine-grained reactivity. This means that only the parts of your application that are affected by a data change are re-rendered. Signals work on a pull-based mechanism, unlike RxJS streams which work on a push-based methodology.

How does a signal work?

Understanding the core mechanism of signals is crucial, as it explains their efficiency and predictability. In essence, a signal operates based on these key principles:

- **Value Container:** A Signal acts like a wrapper or container holding a specific value.
- **Notification on Change:** When the value inside the Signal is updated (using methods like `.set()` or `.update()`), the Signal actively notifies all parts of the application that depend on it (its consumers).
- **Dependency Tracking:** Signals automatically track which parts of your application (like components rendering the value, or computed signals deriving from it) are currently using their value.
- **Targeted Updates:** Because of dependency tracking, when a Signal's value changes, only the specific consumers that were tracked are notified and potentially updated. This avoids unnecessary checks or re-renders in unrelated parts of the application.

This combination of value wrapping, notification, and precise dependency tracking is what enables the fine-grained reactivity and performance benefits of Signals, making rendering efficient and focused.

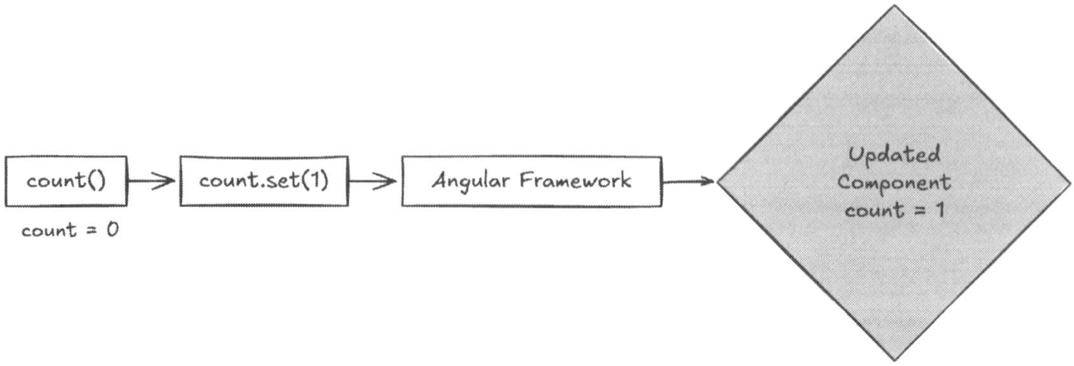

Figure 1.3 - updating the *count* signal updates the Angular framework, which in turn rerenders component

Signals are built around three core building blocks: **`signal()`**, **`computed()`**, and **`effect()`**. In addition to these, you will also learn about **`linkedSignal()`** in this chapter.

signal():

This function is used to create a Signal. A Signal holds a value that can change over time. When you create a signal, you define its initial value. In the code, you will see how you can retrieve the value from the signal, and how you can also update the value.

Example:

```
import { signal } from '@angular/core';
...
class SignalComponent {
  count = signal(0); // Creates a signal with initial value of 0
}
```

You can find the code of this example at `` `apps/chapter-01/src/app/signal` ``. You can follow these commands to see the project:

From the code repository root, run the following:

```
nx serve chapter-01
```

```
# or npx nx serve chapter-01
```

Then, navigate to *http://localhost:4200/signal* to see the example

computed():

Computed signals are derived values based on one or more other signals. When the input signal value(s) change, the computed signal's value is automatically recalculated. They are great for creating derived values from existing signals, which can be used to enhance performance and keep the code cleaner, as computed signals are cached.

Example:

```
import { signal, computed } from '@angular/core';
...
class ComputedComponent {
  price = signal(10);
  quantity = signal(0);
  total = computed(() => this.price() * this.quantity()); //
Creates a computed signal that calculates the total checkout price
  increaseQuantity() {
    this.quantity.update((val) => val + 1);
  }
  decreaseQuantity() {
    this.quantity.update((val) => {
      return val === 0 ? 0 : val - 1;
    });
  }
}
```

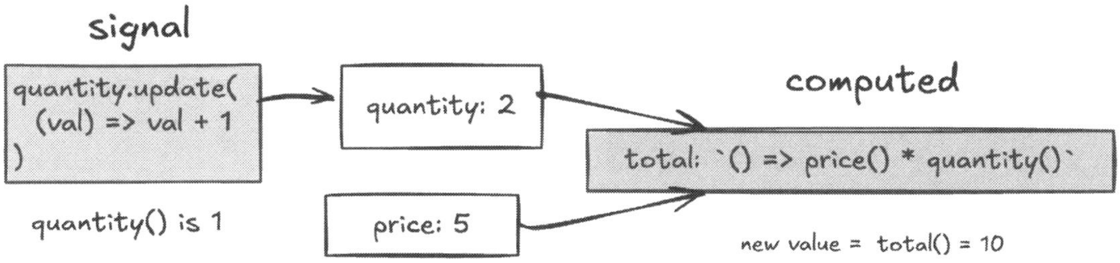

Figure 1.4 - *total* is a computed() signal that updates whenever *quantity* or *price* signals are updated

This example uses a shared component located in the library at **`libs/common-pages/src/lib/computed`**. You can follow these commands to see the project:

From the code repository root, run the following:

```
nx serve chapter-01
# or npx nx serve chapter-01
```

Then, navigate to *http://localhost:4200/computed* to see the example

effect():

This function allows you to perform side effects when a signal value changes. Examples of side effects include updating the DOM, logging to the console, making API calls, and many more. It is very similar to **`useEffect()`** from the React world.

Example:

```
import { signal, effect } from '@angular/core';
...
class EffectComponent {
  count = signal(0);
  countChangeEffect = effect(() => {
    console.log(`count is now: ${this.count()}`);
  });
  increase() {
    this.count.update((val) => val + 1);
  }
  decrease() {
    this.count.update((val) => val - 1);
  }
  // Logs the count value whenever the count signal changes.
}
```

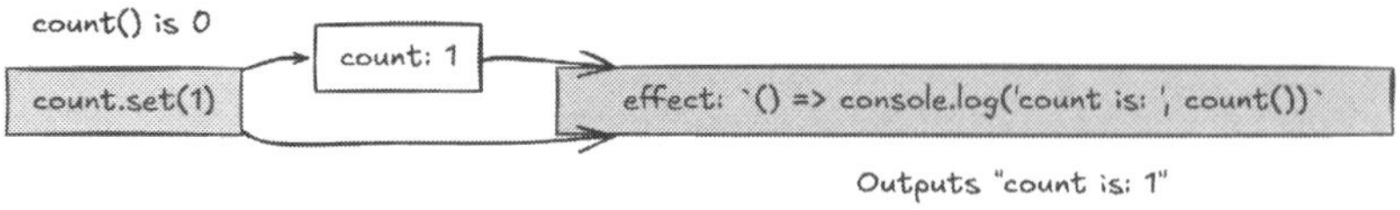

Figure 1.5 - the effect's callback is triggered whenever the value of the *count* signal changes

You can find the code of this example at `apps/chapter-01/src/app/effect`. From the code repository root, run the following command to serve the project:

```
nx serve chapter-01
```

Then, navigate to ***http://localhost:4200/effect*** to see the example

To help solidify the core differences and appropriate uses of these fundamental building blocks (`signal`, `effect`, and `computed`), here's a summary table:

Feature	Purpose	Reactivity	Best Use Case	Return Type
`signal()`	To create a **writable** container for a piece of state that can change over time.	**Source** of reactivity. Notifies consumers when its value is explicitly changed (via `.set()`/`.update()`).	Holding fundamental application state (user input, fetched data, UI flags like visibility).	`WritableSignal<T>` (Allows reading via `()` and writing via `.set()`/`.update()`)
`computed()`	To **derive** a **read-only** value reactively from one or more other signals.	**Reactive Consumer**. Automatically recalculates *only* when dependencies change. Value is memoized (cached).	Creating derived/calculated values without redundant work (e.g., full name, filtered lists, totals, validity).	`Signal<T> (Read-only via ())`
`effect()`	To perform **side effects** (interactions outside state) in reaction to	**Reactive Consumer**. Automatically re-runs its function	Interacting with external systems (DOM manipulation	`EffectRef (Primarily for manual cleanup via .destroy().`

	signals.	whenever dependencies change.	, logging, `localStorage` , triggering data fetches).	`Does not hold state.)`

This table provides a quick reference for understanding when to use each function. `signal()` holds the core state, `computed()` derives new state from existing state efficiently, and `effect()` bridges the gap between your reactive state and the outside world for side effects.

linkedSignal():

LinkedSignal is quite similar to a Computed signal. However, a **`computed()`** signal is read only and you can not modify its value. **`linkedSignal()`** is useful when you want to create a WritableSignal based on one or more signals. For example, if you're using pagination to fetch some data, you may want to reset the page number whenever the search query changes. In this case, instead of creating the page number as a signal, we can use a **`linkedSignal()`** depending on the search query's variable. This way whenever the search query changes, the **`computation()`** method in the LinkedSignal retriggers and sets its value to the returned value from **`computation()`**. And since a LinkedSignal is a **`WriteableSignal`**, you can update its value anytime by calling the **`set()`** or **`update()`** method on it. See the example below.

Example:

```
import { signal, linkedSignal } from '@angular/core';

class LinkedSignalComponent {
  resultsLimit = signal(5);
  searchTerm = signal('');
  resultsPage = linkedSignal({
    source: this.searchTerm,
    computation: () => { // runs whenever search term changes
      return 0;
    }
  });

  nextPage() {
    this.resultsPage.update(page => page + 1);
  }
```

```
  prevPage() {
    this.resultsPage.update(page => page - 1);
  }
}
```

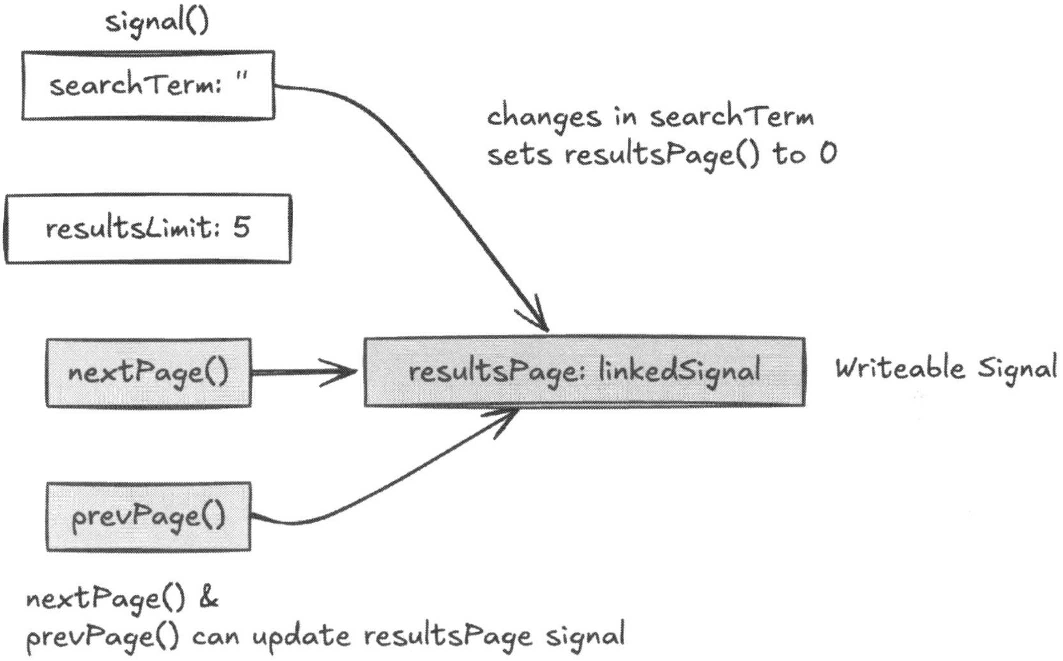

Figure 1.6 – linkedSignal gets set to 0 when *searchTerm* changes. *nextPage* and *prevPage* methods can update the linkedSignal too

You can find the code of this example at `` `apps/chapter-01/src/app/linkedSignal` ``. From the code repository root, run the following command to serve the project:

```
nx serve chapter-01
```

Then, navigate to ***http://localhost:4200/linkedSignal*** to see the example

These three building blocks (`signal()`, `computed()`, and `effect()`) along with `linkedSignal()` form the core of the Angular Signals reactivity model, and you'll be using them to build reactive applications.

Key Terms

To ensure we are all on the same page, let's define the core terms we've introduced:

- `signal`: A container for a value that notifies its consumers when the value changes.
- `computed signal`: A signal whose value is derived from one or more other signals, automatically updated when its dependencies change.
- `effect`: A mechanism to perform side effects when the value of a signal changes.
- `linkedSignal`: A signal that automatically updates when its source signal changes.

These definitions are intended to be concise and are merely to provide clarity on what each of these terms means and we will revisit these concepts in more detail in the subsequent chapters.

Chapter 2: Core Signal Concepts & Building Blocks

Introduction

In the previous chapter, we introduced Angular Signals as a revolutionary approach to managing reactivity in Angular applications. We explored their advantages over traditional methods and touched upon the core building blocks. In this chapter, we'll delve deeper into the heart of Signals, focusing on how to effectively create and use them. We will explore the nuances of **`signal()`**, understand dependency tracking, and lay the foundation for utilizing Signals efficiently in various application scenarios. In addition, we will also touch upon how to create signals in a variety of ways, and what the performance ramifications are. This chapter will also provide practical use-cases and some best practices for using Angular Signals.

Creating Signals: signal() Deep Dive

The **`signal()`** function is the cornerstone of Angular Signals. It's the function you'll use to create a reactive container for a value that can change over time. The **`signal()`** function returns a **`WritableSignal`**, and this function allows you to read, update, and access the value. When you create a **`WritableSignal`** using **`signal()`**, you also need to define its initial value. The initial value could be a simple data type, such as a **`number`**, a **`string`**, or a **`boolean`**. However, it could also be a complex type such as an object or an array. Here are a few examples:

```
import { signal } from '@angular/core';
import { Person } from './types';

class MyComponent {
    // Creating signals with different primitive data types
    count = signal(0); // A number
    message = signal('Hello, Angular!'); // A string
    isActive = signal(true); // A boolean

    // Creating signals with complex data types
    user = signal<Person>({ name: 'John', age: 30 }); // An object
```

```
    items = signal(['item1', 'item2', 'item3']); // An array

    // Creating a signal with null
    initialValueNull = signal(null);

    // Creating a signal with undefined
    initialValueUndefined = signal(undefined);
}
```

As you can see in the code example above, when creating signals you can use any data types that you would typically use in your application. When a signal is created with a value of `null` or `undefined`, you need to be careful while accessing it as TypeScript might not be able to infer the type when used.

To get the value of a signal, you simply call the signal as a function. For example, using `count()` in the HTML template will render the current value of the `count` signal. Similarly, using the `count()` variable in the TypeScript file retrieves the signal's value.

```
import { signal } from '@angular/core';

class MyComponent {
    count = signal(0);

    logCount() {
      console.log(this.count()); // Output: 0
    }
}
```

While using signals is easy, Angular provides mechanisms to easily update the values too. To update the value of a signal, you use either the `set()` method or the `update()` method on it. The `set()` method takes the new value as an argument and replaces the existing value with the new value. The `update()` method, on the other hand, takes a function as an argument. This function receives the existing value and returns the new value, providing functional update capability. We will explore both `set()` and `update()` methods in ***Chapter 4*** in depth.

Here are the examples of updating the value of the signal:

```
import { signal } from '@angular/core';

class MyComponent {
    count = signal(0);

    updateCountUsingSet() {
      this.count.set(1); // Replaces the existing value with 1
      console.log(this.count()); // Output: 1
    }

    updateCountUsingUpdate() {
      // Increments the existing value by 1
      this.count.update((currentCount) => currentCount + 1);
      // Output: 2 (considering the value was 1)
      console.log(this.count());
    }
}
```

Using the **set()** method is quite straightforward, as it replaces the existing value with the new value, but the **update()** method is very helpful for scenarios where the new value depends on the current value, such as incrementing a number, or appending to an array. This approach ensures that you're working with the most up-to-date value.

In addition to using **set()** and **update()**, you can create a **ReadonlySignal** from a **WritableSignal** using the **asReadonly()** method on the signal. This is very useful to encapsulate the logic inside your services, and components to only allow reading the values, while updating them in a specific place, using the **set()** method.

```
import { signal } from '@angular/core';

class MyComponent {
   private _count = signal(0);
   count = this._count.asReadonly();

   logCount() {
     // Reading the readonly signal
     console.log(this.count());
   }
```

```
    updateCount(val: number) {
      this._count.set(val);
    }

    updateReadonlyCount() {
      // This will throw an error - and indicated with squiggly line
even in the editors
      this.count.set(1);
    }
}
```

Using Signals is a very performant way of updating the application as Angular only updates the parts of the component tree that are affected by the change in data. This is what we call ***fine-grained reactivity***, where only the components that are affected by the data changes get re-rendered, and not the entire component tree, as in the case of traditional change detection mechanisms. Signals can be optimized even further, by using `computed()` signals, which we will discuss in the next chapter.

Understanding Dependency Tracking

One of the most powerful features of Angular Signals is their ability to automatically track dependencies. When a `computed()` signal or an `effect()` depends on other signals, Angular creates a ***dependency graph*** and keeps track of it. When a signal is updated, Angular automatically notifies the parts of the application (computed signals, effects, etc) that are dependent on that signal.

To illustrate this, let's consider a practical example. Suppose you have a component that displays a user's full name, which is derived from their first and last names. Here's how you can use dependency tracking:

```
import { signal, computed } from '@angular/core';

class MyComponent {
    firstName = signal('John');
    lastName = signal('Doe');

    fullName = computed(() => `${this.firstName()}
${this.lastName()}`);
```

```
    logFullName() {
        console.log(this.fullName()); // Output: John Doe
        this.firstName.set('Jane');
        console.log(this.fullName()); // Output: Jane Doe
    }
}
```

Let's have a look at a diagram to understand this better:

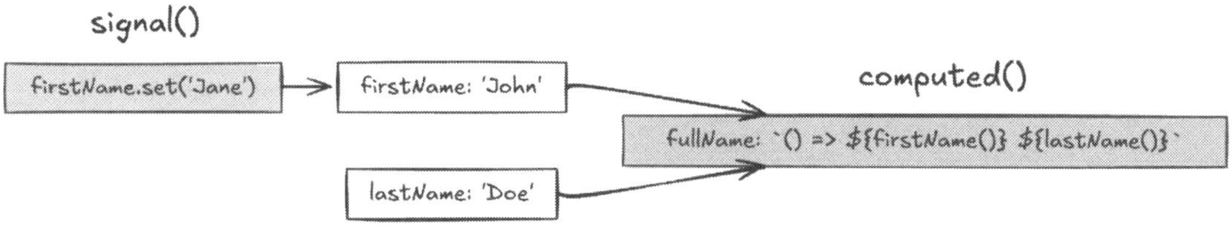

Figure 2.1 - *fullName* is computed again whenever *firstName* and *lastName* signals have a new value

As shown in *Figure 2.1*, **`fullName`** is a computed signal that depends on **`firstName`** and **`lastName`** signals. Angular automatically detects the dependencies and only updates **`fullName`** when **`firstName`** or **`lastName`** changes, and not when some other signal is updated. In other words, Angular does not perform any unnecessary checks, and only updates what is absolutely required.

Now let us think of a more practical scenario. If you're displaying this full name inside your application's component:

```
import { Component, computed, signal } from '@angular/core';

@Component({
  selector: 'app-user-profile',
  imports: [],
  template: `
    <div class="card card-compact bg-base-200 w-96 mx-auto
shadow-xl">
      <div class="card-body flex-col gap-4">
        <h2 class="card-title">User Profile</h2>
```

```
        <div>
          <h1>User Profile</h1>
          <p>Full Name: {{ fullName() }}</p>
        </div>

        <div class="card-actions justify-end">
          <button class="btn btn-primary" (click)="updateName()">
            Update name
          </button>
        </div>
      </div>
    </div>
  `,
  styleUrl: './user-profile.component.scss',
})
export class UserProfileComponent {
  firstName = signal('John');
  lastName = signal('Doe');
  fullName = computed(() => `${this.firstName()}
${this.lastName()}`);

  updateName() {
    this.firstName.set('Muhammad Ahsan');
    this.lastName.set('Ayaz');
  }
}
```

In this example, the component uses a **`computed()`** signal to show the full name. When the firstName is updated using the **`updateName()`** method, only the **`fullName`** is recalculated and the component's template is updated to reflect the change of the full name, without re-rendering other parts of the component. In essence, this is how Signals create an optimized component rendering experience.

You can find the code of this example at `` `apps/chapter-02/src/app/user-profile` ``. You can follow these commands to see the project:

From the code repository root, run the following:

```
nx serve chapter-02
```

```
# or npx nx serve chapter-02
```

Then, navigate to *http://localhost:4200/user-profile* to see the example

This is a big shift from the previous change detection mechanism (as shown in *Figure 1.1*), where Angular would traverse through all components in a tree to check for any changes, even if the component had no change to the data. Signal dependency tracking, and its ability to trigger targeted updates, is a substantial improvement in performance and application complexity.

Practical Use Cases and Scenarios

Signals can be utilized in a variety of application scenarios. Here are some examples:

Managing Component State:

Signals are perfect for managing the state of your components. For example, you might use a signal to control the visibility of a modal:

```
import { Component, signal } from '@angular/core';

@Component({
  selector: 'app-modal-demo',
  templateUrl: './modal-demo.component.html',
})
export class ModalDemoComponent {
  isModalVisible = signal(false);

  toggleModal() {
    this.isModalVisible.update((value) => !value);
  }
}
```

In this example, the `isModalVisible` signal controls the visibility of the modal, and a click on the button will toggle the visibility from shown to hidden, and vice versa.

You can find the code of this example at `apps/chapter-02/src/app/modal-demo`. From the code repository root, run the following command to serve the project:

```
nx serve chapter-02
```

Then, navigate to ***http://localhost:4200/modal-demo*** to see the example

Managing User Input:

Signals are also excellent for managing form fields and user input. Here's an example of how to use a signal for a search query using the **`ngModel`** directive:

```
import { Component, signal } from '@angular/core';
import { FormsModule } from '@angular/forms';

@Component({
  selector: 'app-user-input',
  imports: [FormsModule],
  template: `<input
      type="text"
      [(ngModel)]="searchQuery"
      placeholder="Search..."
      class="input input-bordered"
    />
    <p class="menu">You searched for: {{ searchQuery() }}</p>
  `
})
export class UserInputComponent {
  searchQuery = signal('');
}
```

In this example, the **`searchQuery`** signal holds the value of the search query, and the template displays the search query as the user types into the input field.

You can find the code of this example at `**apps/chapter-02/src/app/user-input**`. From the code repository root, run the following command to serve the project:

```
nx serve chapter-02
```

Then, navigate to ***http://localhost:4200/user-input*** to see the example

Managing Data from an API:

Signals can also manage data that is fetched from an API, with the help of **`resource()`** and **`rxResource()`**, which we will discuss in more detail in subsequent chapters. For now, we'll just use the good old HttpClient to make an API call, and manage the **`loading`**, **`error`**, and data (**`user`**) signals to render the appropriate content.

```
import { afterNextRender, Component, inject, signal } from
'@angular/core';
import { HttpClient } from '@angular/common/http';

type User = {
  ...
};

@Component({
  selector: 'app-managing-api-data',
  template: `<div class="card card-compact bg-base-200 w-96 mx-auto
shadow-xl">
    <div class="card-body flex-col gap-4 min-h-[360px]">
      <h2 class="card-title">Random User</h2>
      @if(loading()) {
      <div class="flex flex-1 justify-between w-full">
        <span class="loading loading-spinner loading-sm
mx-auto"></span>
      </div>
      } @else if(error()) {
      {{ error() }}
      } @else if(user()) {
        <!-- user card here -->
```

```
      }
      <div class="card-actions justify-end">
        <button
          (click)="fetchData()"
          [disabled]="loading()"
          class="btn btn-primary"
        >
          Refresh
        </button>
      </div>
    </div>
  </div> `,
  styles: ``,
})
export class ManagingApiDataComponent {
  user = signal<User | null>(null);
  loading = signal(false);
  error = signal(null);
  httpClient = inject(HttpClient);

  constructor() {
    afterNextRender(() => {
      this.fetchData();
    });
  }

  fetchData() {
    this.loading.set(true);
    this.httpClient
      .get<{ results: User[] }>('https://randomuser.me/api')
      .subscribe({
        next: (res) => {
          this.user.set(res.results[0]);
          this.loading.set(false);
          this.error.set(null);
        },
        error: (err) => {
          this.error.set(err.message);
          this.loading.set(false);
          this.user.set(null);
        },
```

```
        });
    }
}
```

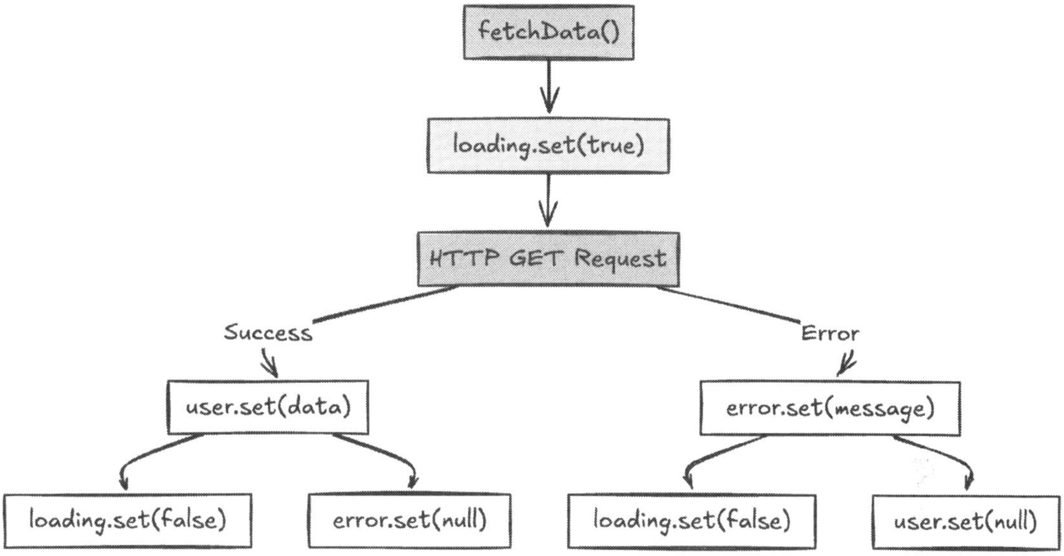

Figure 2.2 - *loading, error,* and *user* signals to handle API responses

As shown in *Figure 2.2*, in this example we are using 3 signals for loading state, error state, and data (user information) from the API. These are just simple examples, and we will explore how to use signals with async data using **`resource`** and **`rxResource`** in subsequent chapters.

You can find the code of this example at **`apps/chapter-02/src/app/managing-api-data`**. From the code repository root, run the following command to serve the project:

```
nx serve chapter-02
```

Then, navigate to ***http://localhost:4200/managing-api-data*** to see the example

Best Practices

Here are some best practices for working with Signals:

- **Keep Signals Focused:** Create signals for specific values that change independently. If multiple related values change together, consider creating a single signal for a complex object.
- **Use set() and update() appropriately:** Use `set()` for direct replacement and `update()` for functional updates based on current values.
- **Lifecycle Management:** Be mindful of the lifecycle of signals, especially in effects and complex components. Unsubscribe or clean up if necessary to prevent memory leaks (though this is not an issue for signals).
- **Avoid Overuse:** Don't use signals where a simple variable would suffice. Use signals only when you need reactive capabilities.
- **Use asReadonly():** Use the `.asReadonly()` method to create a readonly signal, which makes your code predictable and safer to modify.

Conclusion

In this chapter, we explored the core concepts of Angular Signals and their basic building block `signal()`. You learned how to create signals, read and update their values, and how Angular automatically tracks dependencies. You also learned how the concept of dependency tracking makes Angular a more performant framework to develop applications with. We also explored some practical use-cases where signals can be used in various application scenarios. In the next chapter, we'll dive into the world of `computed()` signals, exploring how to derive values from existing signals and enhance your application's performance even further.

Chapter 3: Mastering Computed Signals and Effects

Introduction

In the previous chapter, we explored the fundamental building block of Angular Signals, the `signal()`, and how to create signals to manage state and track dependencies. Now, we will introduce `computed()` and `effect()`, two powerful tools for building highly responsive and optimized Angular applications. `computed()` allows you to create derived values from existing signals, and `effect()` allows you to perform side effects when the values of signals change. Together, they are vital for creating complex and efficient reactive applications.

computed() Signals: Deep Dive

The `computed()` function is used to create a computed signal. A computed signal is a *read-only* signal that derives its value from one or more other signals. It takes a function as its only argument. This function is then used to compute the value of the *computed* signal. The computed signal then tracks which signals were read during the execution of this function. Whenever any of these dependent signals change, the computed signal is automatically re-evaluated, and its new value is updated. The power of `computed()` comes from its ability to derive complex values while ensuring that those computations only happen when necessary.

Let us explore the following example, where a computed signal derives its value from other signals:

```
import { Component, signal, computed } from '@angular/core';

@Component({
    selector: 'app-computed-demo',
    template: `
      <button class="btn btn-square btn-sm"
(click)="decreaseQuantity()">
        -
      </button>
      <span class="text-xl">{{ quantity() }}</span
      ><button (click)="increaseQuantity()" class="btn btn-square
```

```
btn-sm">
        +
      </button>
    `
})
export class ComputedDemoComponent {
  price = signal(10);
  quantity = signal(0);
  total = computed(() => this.price() * this.quantity()); //
Creates a computed signal that calculates the total checkout price
  increaseQuantity() {
    this.quantity.update((val) => val + 1);
  }
  decreaseQuantity() {
    this.quantity.update((val) => {
      return val === 0 ? 0 : val - 1;
    });
  }
}
```

In this example, the `total` signal is a computed signal that is derived from the `price` and the `quantity` signals. Whenever the `price` or the `quantity` signal is updated, the `total` signal is automatically recalculated. It is essential to know that the `total` is a read-only signal, which means you cannot directly update its value by using `set()`. Instead, you can only update its value by updating its *dependent* signals `price` or `quantity`.

> This example uses a shared component located in the library at `` `libs/common-pages/src/lib/computed` ``. From the code repository root, run the following command to serve the project:
>
> **`nx serve chapter-03`**
>
> Then, navigate to ***http://localhost:4200/computed*** to see the example

A core feature of `computed()` is its built-in *memoization* and *caching*. When a `computed()` signal is first accessed, it executes its function to calculate the derived value. The value is then *cached*. Subsequent accesses of the signal do not re-evaluate the function, provided that the dependent signals have not changed. This caching behavior can drastically improve performance for expensive calculations that depend on the values from other signals. The **computed()** signal is only re-evaluated when its *dependent* signals change.

For example, if you fetch an object from an API and transform the data to be used in your UI, the **computed()** signal can cache the transformed object so that it does not re-evaluate for all the renders.

Here is a more realistic example, where **computed()** is used to derive a value for a filtered list:

```
import { Component, computed, signal } from '@angular/core';
import { randFullName } from '@ngneat/falso';
import { FormsModule } from '@angular/forms';

@Component({
  selector: 'app-computed-filter',
  template: `
    <input
      [(ngModel)]="searchTerm"
      placeholder="search..."
      class="input input-bordered w-full max-w-xs"
    />
    <div>
      <ul class="menu">
        @for (person of filtered(); track $index) {
          <li>
            <a>{{ person }}</a>
          </li>
        }
      </ul>
    </div>
  `,
  imports: [FormsModule],
})
export class ComputedFilterComponent {
  searchTerm = signal('');
  resultsLimit = signal(5);
  people = signal(
    randFullName({
      length: 20,
    })
  );
```

```
  filtered = computed(() => {
    if (!this.searchTerm().trim()) {
      return this.people();
    }
    return this.people().filter((name) => {
      return
name.toLowerCase().includes(this.searchTerm().toLowerCase());
    });
  });
}
```

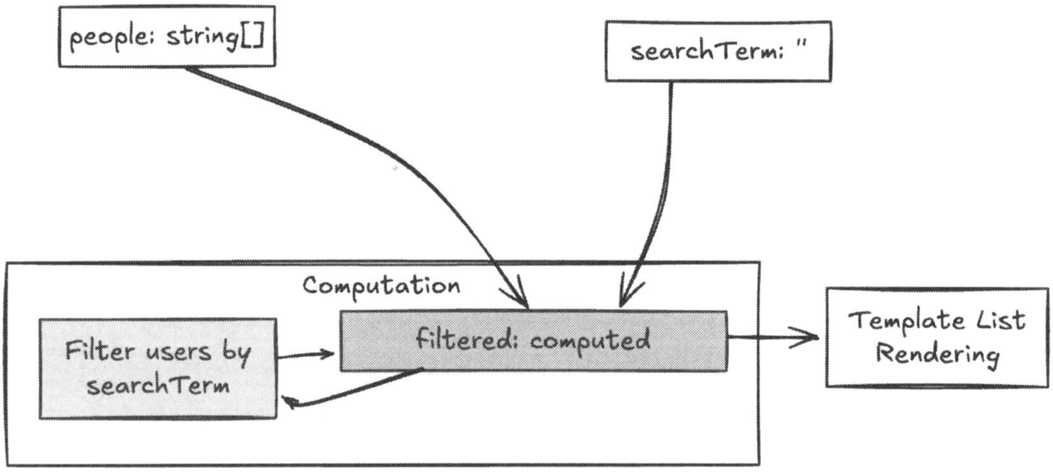

Figure 3.1 - *filteredItems* recalculates when the *searchTerm* or *item* signal gets updated

As shown in *Figure 3.1*, in this example, the **`filteredItems`** signal will only recalculate when the **`searchTerm`** signal or the **`items`** signal is updated. Any other updates that may happen in the component will not cause the filteredItems to recalculate. This makes the application performant and makes code easier to maintain.

> You can find the code of this example at **`` `apps/chapter-03/src/app/computed-filter` ``**. From the code repository root, run the following command to serve the project:
>
> **`nx serve chapter-03`**

Then, navigate to ***http://localhost:4200/computed-filter*** to see the example

effect() Signals: Deep Dive

The `effect()` function allows you to perform side effects when the values of one or more signals change. It accepts a *function* as an argument. An effect is essentially a piece of code that runs automatically whenever any of its dependent signals are updated within the provided *function*. Side effects include tasks like updating the DOM, logging to the console, making API calls, setting timeouts, etc. Unlike computed signals, which derive and cache a value, the function in `effect()` does not return a value; it simply executes code when its dependencies change. It is somewhat similar to the `useEffect` hook from the React world. However, the `effect()` function itself returns an `EffectRef` which can be used to destroy the effect using the `.destroy()` method on it.

Let us explore some common use-cases for effects.

The following example shows how to use `effect` to log changes to a signal value:

```
import { Component, effect, OnDestroy, signal } from
'@angular/core';

@Component({
  selector: 'lib-effect',
  imports: [],
  templateUrl: './effect.component.html',
  styleUrl: './effect.component.scss',
})
export class EffectComponent implements OnDestroy {
  count = signal(0);
  countChangeEffect = effect(() => {
    console.log(`count is now: ${this.count()}`);
  });
  increase() {
    this.count.update((val) => val + 1);
  }
  decrease() {
    this.count.update((val) => val - 1);
```

```
  }
  checkValue() {
    alert(`count is now: ${this.count()}`);
  }

  ngOnDestroy(): void {
    this.countChangeEffect.destroy();
  }
}
```

In this example, the `countChangeEffect` is automatically called when the `count` signal is changed.

This example uses a shared component located in the library at `` `libs/common-pages/src/lib/effect` ``. From the code repository root, run the following command to serve the project:

`nx serve chapter-03`

Then, navigate to ***http://localhost:4200/effect*** to see the example

The `effect()` signal will also trigger when it is first created, as the signal is initially set up and the code is evaluated. Therefore, whenever you create an effect, make sure that you are handling the first run case, where it may not necessarily be due to signal change. The dependency tracking inside effect also works similar to computed signals, so it only executes when its *dependent* signals change.

Here is another example of an effect performing **DOM manipulation**:

```
import {
  Component,
  ElementRef,
  signal,
  effect,
  viewChild,
  afterNextRender,
} from '@angular/core';
```

```
@Component({
  selector: 'app-effect-dom-demo',
  template: `
    ...
  `,
  styles: [
    `...`,
  ],
})
export class EffectDomDemoComponent {
  boxRef = viewChild.required<
    ElementRef<HTMLDivElement>
  >('box');
  /**
   * Whether the box is currently rotating.
   * Toggling this will start/stop the effect.
   */
  rotating = signal(false);

  /**
   * The current rotation angle of the box (in degrees).
   */
  angle = signal(0);

  /**
   * Effect that updates the box's transform style whenever
   * `rotating` or `angle` changes.
   */
  rotationEffect = effect(() => {
    if (!this.boxRef()) return;

    const boxEl = this.boxRef().nativeElement;

    if (this.rotating()) {
      // Rotate based on the current angle
      boxEl.style.transform = `rotate(${this.angle()}deg)`;
    } else {
      // Reset rotation
      boxEl.style.transform = 'rotate(0deg)';
      this.angle.set(0);
```

```
    }
  });

  constructor() {
    afterNextRender(() => {
      // Increment the angle every half second if rotating = true
      setInterval(() => {
        if (this.rotating()) {
          this.angle.update((prev) => (prev + 15) % 360);
        }
      }, 500);
    });
  }

  toggleRotation() {
    this.rotating.update((prev) => !prev);
  }
}
```

In this example, the **`effect()`** will update the **`transform`** style of the box based on whether rotating is true or false. If **`rotating`** is **`true`**, the box's rotation will be set to the current angle (in degrees). If **`rotating`** is **`false`**, the **`transform`** is reset to **`rotate(0deg)`**, and the **`angle`** is set to zero. The approach uses **`viewChild.required('box')`** to reference the box element within the component, improving encapsulation.

You can find the code of this example at **`` `apps/chapter-03/src/app/effect-dom-demo` ``**. From the code repository root, run the following command to serve the project:

`nx serve chapter-03`

Then, navigate to ***http://localhost:4200/effect-dom-demo*** to see the example

Another important aspect of using **`effect()`** is managing lifecycle and cleanup operations. In Angular, an effect is destroyed when its *enclosing context* is destroyed. For example, within a directive, component, or service. However, in some scenarios, you may not want the effect anymore during the lifecycle of the enclosing context. In which case, you can use the **`.destroy()`** method on the **`EffectRef`** manually.

Here's an example of how to use cleanup with **`effect`**:

```
import { Component, signal, effect, EffectRef } from
'@angular/core';

@Component({
  selector: 'app-effect-cleanup',
  template: `...`,
})
export class EffectCleanupComponent {
  counter = signal(0);
  private loggerEffect: EffectRef;

  constructor() {
    this.loggerEffect = effect((onCleanup) => {
      console.log(`Counter changed to: ${this.counter()}`);

      onCleanup(() => {
        console.log('🧹 Cleanup function executed');
      });
    });
  }

  increment() {
    this.counter.update((c) => c + 1);
  }

  stopLogger() {
    this.loggerEffect.destroy();
    console.log('🛑 Effect manually destroyed');
  }
}
```

In this example, **`loggerEffect`** is defined with an **`onCleanup`** callback that logs a message whenever the effect is cleaned up. The effect itself prints the new counter value whenever **`counter()`** changes. When you click the "**Stop Logger**" button, the **`loggerEffect`** is manually destroyed, triggering the cleanup function (which logs the "*🧹 Cleanup function executed*" message). Cleanup is also automatically invoked if the component is destroyed or if *dependencies* in the effect change, demonstrating how an effect's lifecycle can be managed both automatically and via explicit calls to `destroy()`.

> You can find the code of this example at `` `apps/chapter-03/src/app/effect-cleanup` ``. From the code repository root, run the following command to serve the project:
>
> ```
> nx serve chapter-03
> ```
>
> Then, navigate to ***http://localhost:4200/effect-cleanup*** to see the example

Figure 3.2 shows the process's flow of the effect, with respect to the component's lifecycle:

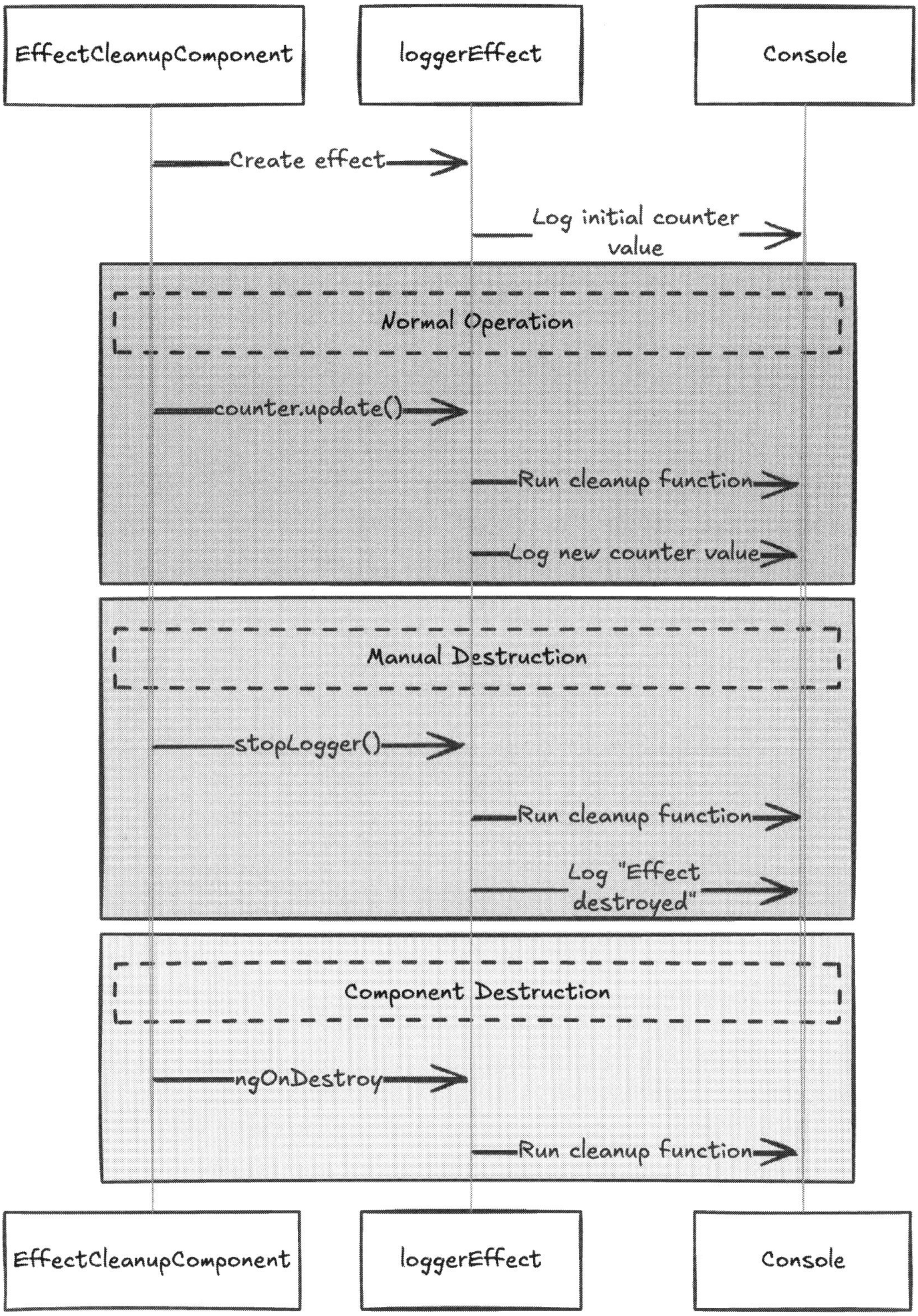

Figure 3.2 - creation, execution, and cleanup of the effect w.r.t component lifecycle

Advanced Patterns and Techniques

Here are some advanced patterns that you can use with `computed()` and `effect()` together:

- **Creating Reactive State:** You can use computed signals to create dynamic reactive states based on conditional logic. You can have multiple signals influencing another computed signal, and you can have conditions inside the computed block based on other signal values.
- **Handling Multiple API Calls:** Using effects along with `resource` (which we will discuss in subsequent chapters), you can make API calls based on other signals, and all of the responses can be *cached* using the resource.
- **Reactive Data Grid:** You can create a complex data grid where filtering, sorting, and other operations are derived with `computed` signals. If you need to perform side effects with any of the updates, then you can always use an `effect` too.
- **Debouncing a Value:** When handling user inputs, you can use effects along with timers to debounce a value. The timer inside the effect can be used to only trigger an action after a certain period, and with proper cleanup, you can make sure that you are only running the effect once.

Complex Project Example Ideas

- **A Real-Time Dashboard:** This project would involve fetching data from a backend API and displaying real-time updates on a dashboard. `computed()` could be used for calculations and aggregations, while `effect()` could handle updating the UI based on changes in the data and also making API calls. This will be a very powerful and performant project if implemented with Angular Signals.
- **A Dynamic Form:** Build a dynamic form where form fields and their behavior change based on user inputs using `computed()` and `effect()`. The `computed()` could be used to show or hide a form field based on another form field's input, while `effect()` can be used to perform asyncronous form validation and other such tasks.
- **A Feature-Rich Data Grid:** You can build a feature-rich data grid where the data can be filtered, sorted, and paginated using computed signals. The `effect()` can be used to make API calls to fetch data and perform other UI updates.

Conclusion

In this chapter, we dove deep into `computed()` and `effect()`, two essential components of the Angular Signals model. You've learned how `computed()` enables you to derive values in a performant way and how to use `effect()` to perform side effects while being aware of the importance of cleanup. These functions will greatly help in building complex and efficient Angular applications. We also looked at some complex use cases, and project ideas that can be built using these two powerful functions. In the next chapter, we'll explore how to manage signal mutations, and the best ways to update the values of signals in various scenarios.

Chapter 4: Signal Mutations and Updates

Introduction

In the previous chapters, we established a strong understanding of Angular Signals, covering their core building blocks and use-cases. Now, it is crucial to dive deeper into how you can efficiently update the values of signals, which is referred to as signal mutation. In this chapter, we will explore the nuances of updating signal values, and the different strategies involved. We will learn about `set()` and `update()`, and when to use each method. We will also explore how to handle updating complex data structures such as objects and arrays and the strategies for optimizing signal mutations. Understanding signal mutations will enable you to write robust, predictable and performant Angular applications.

Updating Signal Values

Angular Signals provide two primary methods for updating the value of a WritableSignal: `set()` and `update()`. While both methods modify the signal's value, they differ in how they accomplish this and provide different benefits, so it is important to know when to use each method.

The `set()` method is straightforward: it directly replaces the current value of the signal with a new value. You pass the new value as an argument to `set()`, and it immediately updates the signal. Here's a simple example:

```
import { Component, signal } from '@angular/core';

@Component({
  selector: 'app-set-example',
  template: `
    <p>Count: {{count()}}</p>
    <button (click)="setCount()">Set Count</button>
  `
})
export class SetExampleComponent {
  count = signal(0);
```

```
  setCount() {
    this.count.set(5); // Direct replacement of existing value with
5
  }
}
```

In the example above, when the button is clicked, the value of the `count` signal will change from `0` to `5`. The template will then update to show the updated value.

While the `set()` method is straightforward to use, there are scenarios where using the `update()` method can offer more control and avoid some potential issues. The `update()` method uses a functional update pattern where instead of taking the new value directly, it takes a function as an argument. This function takes the current value of the signal and returns the new value, as shown in the example below:

```
import { Component, signal } from '@angular/core';

@Component({
    selector: 'app-update-example',
    template: `
        <p>Count: {{count()}}</p>
        <button (click)="incrementCount()">Increment Count</button>
    `
})
export class UpdateExampleComponent {
    count = signal(0);

    incrementCount() {
        // updates the current count value by adding 1
        this.count.update(currentCount => currentCount + 1);
    }
}
```

In the above example, when the button is clicked, the count signal value is updated by using the `update()` function and the value is incremented by `1`.

The `update()` method is incredibly useful when the new value is dependent on the current value. It helps prevent race conditions that can happen with multiple updates and ensures that you are always working with the correct value. Additionally, the `update()` method is essential when working with complex data structures such as objects and arrays, and we will explore this further in the next section.

Working with Complex Data Structures

When working with signals that hold complex data structures such as objects and arrays, you need to be extra careful. Directly mutating objects and arrays within a signal will lead to unexpected behavior. Angular Signals track dependencies by reference, so if you modify the reference to an object or array without creating a new object, then Angular may not detect the change in the value.

Instead of modifying data directly, you should use the `update()` method to create new copies of your data structures with updated values, while retaining the existing values in the original object or array. This helps you adhere to the concept of immutability, and ensures that Angular detects the change.

Let's illustrate this with an example – a dynamic shopping cart for fruits 🍎🍊🍌:

```
import { CurrencyPipe } from '@angular/common';
import { Component, signal, computed } from '@angular/core';

interface CartItem {
  name: string;
  emoji: string;
  quantity: number;
  price: number;
}

@Component({
  selector: 'app-dynamic-shopping-cart',
  imports: [CurrencyPipe],
  template: `
    <h2>Shopping Cart 🛒</h2>
    <button (click)="addToCart('apple')">Add Apple 🍎</button>
    <button (click)="addToCart('orange')">Add Orange 🍊</button>
    <button (click)="addToCart('banana')">Add Banana 🍌</button>
```

```
    <p>Total Items: {{ totalItems() }}</p>
    <p>Total Price: {{ totalPrice() | currency }}</p>
    <ul>
      @for (item of cart(); track item) {
      <li>
        {{ item.name }} {{ item.emoji }} x {{ item.quantity }} -
        {{ item.price * item.quantity | currency }}
        <button (click)="remove(item)">Remove</button>
        <input
          type="number"
          [value]="item.quantity"
          (change)="updateQuantity($event, item)"
        />
      </li>
      }
    </ul>
  `,
})
export class DynamicShoppingCartComponent {
  cart = signal<CartItem[]>([]);

  totalItems = computed(() =>
    this.cart().reduce((acc, curr) => acc + curr.quantity, 0)
  );

  totalPrice = computed(() =>
    this.cart().reduce((acc, curr) => acc + curr.quantity *
curr.price, 0)
  );

  addToCart(fruitName: string) {
    this.cart.update((items) => {
      const existingItem = items.find((i) => i.name === fruitName);
      if (existingItem) {
        return items.map((item) => {
          if (item.name === fruitName) {
            return { ...item, quantity: item.quantity + 1 };
          }
          return item;
        });
      }
```

```
      const newItem: CartItem = {
        name: fruitName,
        emoji:
          fruitName === 'apple' ? '🍎' : fruitName === 'orange' ?
'🍊' : '🍌',
        quantity: 1,
        price: fruitName === 'apple' ? 1 : fruitName === 'orange' ?
1.2 : 0.8,
      };
      return [...items, newItem];
    });
  }

  remove(itemToRemove: CartItem) {
    this.cart.update((items) => items.filter((item) => item !==
itemToRemove));
  }

  updateQuantity(event: any, itemToUpdate: CartItem) {
    this.cart.update((items) =>
      items.map((item) => {
        if (item === itemToUpdate) {
          return { ...item, quantity: parseInt(event.target.value,
10) };
        }
        return item;
      })
    );
  }
}
```

In this example, we use a cart signal to hold an array of cart items. The `addToCart` function updates this cart by using the `update` method. If an item exists in the cart, the quantity is updated. If not, a new item is added to the cart. The remove method uses the `Array` class's `filter` method to create a **new array** without the item that needs to be removed, while the `updateQuantity` is used to change the quantity of an item inside the cart. You will also notice that in the `updateQuantity` method, we are using `items.map()` which returns a new array as well. All of the updates here are using functional array updates, and they adhere to the immutability pattern. You will also notice that we are using `@for` loop instead of `ngFor`.

Note: This is a simplified example which shows the functionality and the template. Refer to a practical (and nicer) implementation in the codebase in the app for Chapter 4, as shared below.

You can find the code of this example at `` `apps/chapter-04/src/app/dynamic-shopping-cart` ``. From the code repository root, run the following command to serve the project:

```
nx serve chapter-04
```

Then, navigate to ***http://localhost:4200/dynamic-shopping-cart*** to see the example

Similarly, consider the weather example. To update the weather data, we need to be very careful to avoid direct mutation, while also managing loading and error state:

```
import { Component, signal } from '@angular/core';

interface WeatherData {
  temperature: number;
  condition: string;
  icon: string;
}

@Component({
  selector: 'app-weather-info',
  template: `
    <div class="flex flex-col items-center gap-4">
      <button class="btn btn-primary btn-outline"
(click)="fetchWeather()">
        Fetch Weather
      </button>
      @if (loading()) {
      <div>Loading...</div>
      } @else if (error()) {
      <div>Error: {{ error() }}</div>
      } @else if (weatherData()) {
```

```
      <img
        [src]="weatherData()?.icon"
        class="w-20 object-fit"
        alt="weather icon"
      />
      <p>Temperature: {{ weatherData()?.temperature }}</p>
      <p>Condition: {{ weatherData()?.condition }}</p>
      }
    </div>
  `,
})
export class WeatherInfoComponent {
  weatherData = signal<WeatherData | null>(null);
  loading = signal(false);
  error = signal<string | null>(null);

  async fetchWeather() {
    this.loading.set(true);
    try {
      const response = await new Promise<Response>((resolve) => {
        setTimeout(() => {
          fetch('assets/weather.json').then((r) => resolve(r));
        }, 1500);
      });
      if (!response.ok) {
        throw new Error('Could not fetch data');
      }
      const data = await response.json();

      this.weatherData.set(data);
      this.error.set(null);
    } catch (err) {
      this.error.set((err as Error).message);
      this.weatherData.set(null);
    } finally {
      this.loading.set(false);
    }
  }
}
```

In this example, we are showing how to update the value of the **`weatherData`** signal, after a response from an API has been received. We also handle the `loading` state and the `error` state too, in a functional manner. We never update the object (`weatherData`) directly, but rather using the `set` method.

You can find the code of this example at `apps/chapter-04/src/app/weather-info`. From the code repository root, run the following command to serve the project:

```
nx serve chapter-04
```

Then, navigate to ***http://localhost:4200/weather-info*** to see the example

Strategies for Optimizing Signal Mutations

In addition to correctly updating the signal values, there are several other techniques you can use to optimize the mutations:

- **Minimize Unnecessary Updates:** Ensure you update the value of a signal only when necessary. If you are updating several different signals, you might need to perform batch updates where you only update a signal when a certain threshold is reached. This can prevent excessive renders.
- **Use Computed Signals:** You should use computed signals to derive values when a derived value is needed. This helps with performance, as it caches the computed value, and only re-evaluates when the dependencies change. In our shopping cart example, we are using computed signals to calculate total items and price.
- **Use update() for Complex Logic:** When performing complex updates use the `update()` method with conditional logic in the update function. This allows you to combine the update logic with the value retrieval, and perform it all in a single place.

Practical Use-Cases

Here are some practical examples of how you can manage signal mutations in real-world scenarios:

Interactive Recipe List:

Building on our earlier idea, we can use signals to create an interactive recipe list where ingredients can be checked off, and the UI is updated accordingly. You can also use computed signals for deriving the total number of items that are checked, etc.

User Settings with Theme Switcher:

You can use signals to hold user preferences, such as dark mode setting, and apply theme updates to your application using effect().

Countdown Timer:

Use the update method along with intervals to update the value of the countdown timer. You can use an effect along with a cleanup mechanism to ensure that you unsubscribe to the timer when it is no longer needed.

Conclusion

In this chapter, we explored various methods for signal mutations. We explored the differences between `set()` and `update()`, and when to use them. We also explored strategies to handle updates with complex data structures such as objects and arrays, and the importance of immutability. We also discussed briefly about how to optimize signal mutations using various techniques to minimize unnecessary updates. In the next chapter, we will explore `resource` and `rxResource` and learn how to work with asynchronous operations using signals.

Chapter 5: Resource Management with Signals

Introduction

In previous chapters, we explored the core building blocks of Angular Signals and how to use them for managing state, deriving values, and updating them correctly. In this chapter, we will delve into *asynchronous operations* and explore the powerful APIs that Angular Signals provides for managing them: `resource()` & `rxResource()`. We'll investigate how these features handle ***asynchronous data fetching, loading states, errors***, and reacting to ***changes*** in related signal values. Understanding resource management is essential for building high-quality, reactive Angular applications.

Basic Resource Fetching

Angular's `resource()` method provides a straightforward way to handle asynchronous data fetching. Let's start with the most basic scenario: fetching weather data for a single city using `resource`. This will create the foundation for more advanced techniques.

We'll define a resource that fetches data, and have a button that *fetches* the data again whenever clicked. We'll also display the ***loading*** state and *weather information* once the data is loaded.

Here's the initial component code:

```
import { Component, resource } from '@angular/core';

interface WeatherData {
  temperature: number;
  condition: string;
  icon: string;
}

@Component({
  selector: 'app-weather-info',
  template: `
    <div class="card bg-base-200 w-96 shadow-xl mx-auto">
      <div class="card-body flex flex-col items-center gap-4">
        <button
          class="btn btn-block btn-primary btn-outline"
```

```
        (click)="weatherResource.reload()"
      >
        Get Weather Info
      </button>
      @if (weatherResource.isLoading()) {
        <span class="loading loading-spinner loading-lg"></span>
      } @else if (weatherResource.value()) {
        <img
          [src]="weatherResource.value()?.icon"
          class="w-20 object-fit"
          alt="weather icon"
        />
        <p class="text-2xl">
          Temperature: {{ weatherResource.value()?.temperature }}
        </p>
        <p class="text-xl">
          Condition: {{ weatherResource.value()?.condition }}
        </p>
      }
    </div>
  </div>
  `,
})
export class WeatherInfoComponent {
  weatherResource = resource<WeatherData, string>({
    loader: async ({ abortSignal }) => {
      const response = await new Promise<Response>((resolve) => {
        setTimeout(() => {
          fetch('assets/weather.json', { signal: abortSignal
}).then((r) =>
            resolve(r)
          );
        }, 1500);
      });
      if (!response.ok) {
        throw new Error('Could not fetch data');
      }
      const data = await response.json();
      return data as WeatherData;
    },
  });
```

```
}
```

In this component, we are using the **`resource`** function to fetch data asynchronously. Let's break down the code:

- We are using the **`resource`** function to fetch data.
- The **`loader`** function is an async function that uses a **`setTimeout`** to simulate a delay, before fetching data from the **`assets/weather.json`** file.
- The **`abortSignal`** is used to cancel the request when the component is destroyed or when a request is cancelled.
- The **`template`** displays the weather data, once the resource has completed *loading*, or an *error* message, if the data fetch fails.
- The **`weatherResource.reload()`** is used to trigger the data fetch again.

> You can find the code of this example at **`` `apps/chapter-05/src/app/weather-info-simple` ``**. From the code repository root, run the following command to serve the project:
>
> **`nx serve chapter-05`**
>
> Then, navigate to ***http://localhost:4200/weather-info-simple*** to see the example

Figure 5.1 shows the process of the component loading the weather information data from the API call, via **`resource()`**:

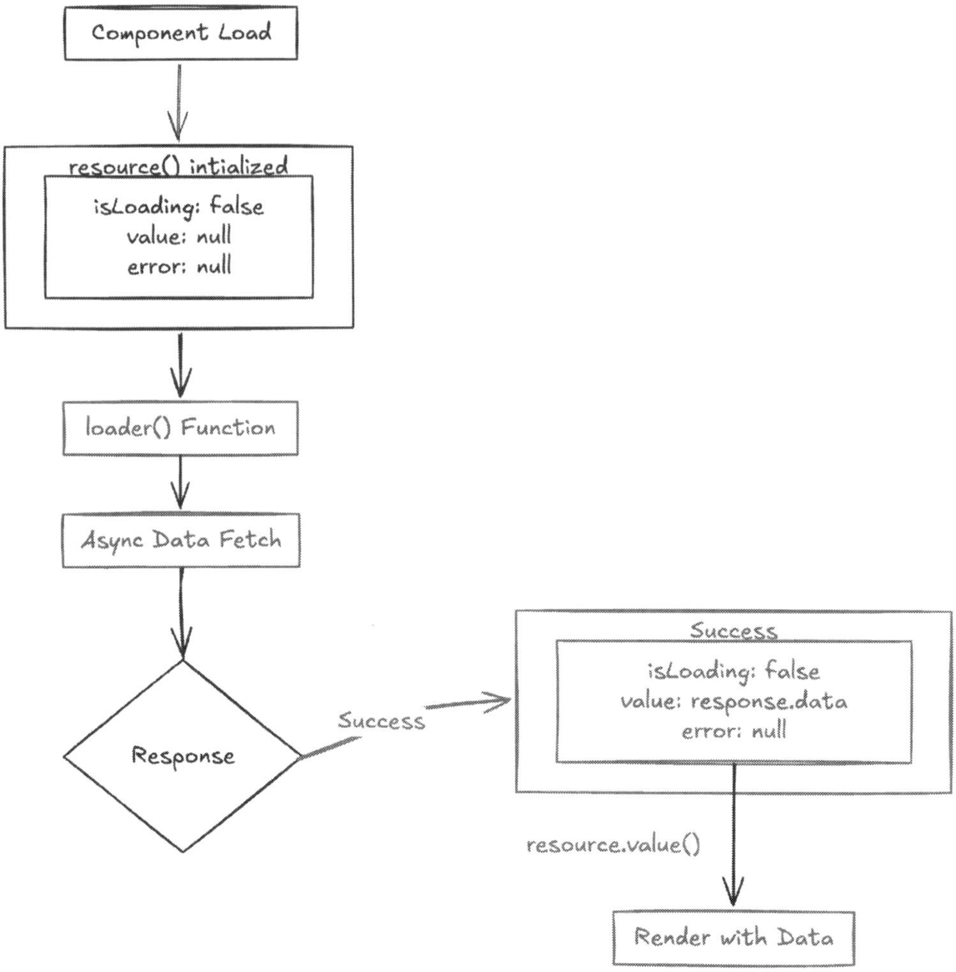

Figure 5.1 - weather info component's process for fetching data via the *resource* API

The **`resource()`** method simplifies asynchronous data fetching by managing the loading state, handling errors, and providing the data once it has been loaded, and makes the component reactive to changes in data.

Loading Resources On-Demand

In the previous example, the ***resource*** was initialized immediately when the component was created, triggering a data fetch. What if you want to defer this fetch until a specific action? You can use the **`params`** attribute to control *when* the resource's loader is executed, allowing you to load resources on-demand.

Let's modify our previous example to include a **`weatherRequestState`** signal. This signal will determine if the resource's **`loader`** should be triggered. This way, we can load our ***resource*** on-demand based on user interactions.

Here's the updated code:

```
import { Component, resource, signal } from '@angular/core';

interface WeatherData {
  temperature: number;
  condition: string;
  icon: string;
}

type WeatherRequestState = 'idle' | 'ready';

@Component({
  selector: 'app-weather-info',
  template: `
    <div class="card bg-base-200 w-96 shadow-xl mx-auto">
      <div class="card-body flex flex-col items-center gap-4">
        <button class="btn btn-block btn-primary btn-outline"
(click)="getWeatherInfo()">
          Fetch Weather
        </button>
        @if (weatherResource.isLoading()) {
          <span class="loading loading-spinner loading-lg"></span>
        } @else if (weatherResource.value()) {
          <img
            [src]="weatherResource.value()?.icon"
            class="w-20 object-fit"
            alt="weather icon"
          />
          <p class="text-2xl">
            Temperature: {{ weatherResource.value()?.temperature }}
          </p>
          <p class="text-xl">
            Condition: {{ weatherResource.value()?.condition }}
          </p>
        }
      </div>
    </div>
  `,
```

```
})
export class WeatherInfoComponent {
  weatherRequestState = signal<WeatherRequestState>('idle');
  weatherResource = resource<WeatherData, WeatherRequestState |
undefined>({
    params: () => {
      if (this.weatherRequestState() === 'idle') {
        return undefined;
      }
      return this.weatherRequestState();
    },
    loader: async ({ abortSignal }) => {
      const response = await new Promise<Response>((resolve) => {
        setTimeout(() => {
          fetch('assets/weather.json', { signal: abortSignal
}).then((r) =>
            resolve(r)
          );
        }, 1500);
      });
      if (!response.ok) {
        throw new Error('Could not fetch data');
      }
      const data = await response.json();
      return data as WeatherData;
    },
  });

  getWeatherInfo() {
    if (this.weatherRequestState() !== 'ready') {
      this.weatherRequestState.set('ready');
    } else {
      this.weatherResource.reload();
    }
  }
}
```

In this example, we are using a **`weatherRequestState`** signal to control when the resource should load. The state can be **`'idle'`** or **`'ready'`**. Let's discuss this further:

- We've introduced a **`weatherRequestState`** signal, which controls when the loader function is called.
- The **`params`** method is used to control the loader, by setting the value to **`undefined`**, when the **`weatherRequestState`** is idle, thus avoiding the initial data fetch.
- The loader function will only be called when the **`params`** function returns a value other than **`undefined`**.
- The **`getWeatherInfo()`** method sets the **`weatherRequestState`** to **`'ready'`** which then triggers a data fetch using the **`loader`** method. We have also provided a condition that uses the **`reload`** method on the resource, if the **`weatherRequestState`** is not idle, so that when the user clicks the button again, then a data fetch will be re-triggered.

> You can find the code of this example at **`` `apps/chapter-05/src/app/weather-info-on-demand` ``**. From the code repository root, run the following command to serve the project:
>
> **`nx serve chapter-05`**
>
> Then, navigate to ***http://localhost:4200/weather-info-on-demand*** to see the example

Figure 5.2 shows the flow on how we load resource on user interaction:

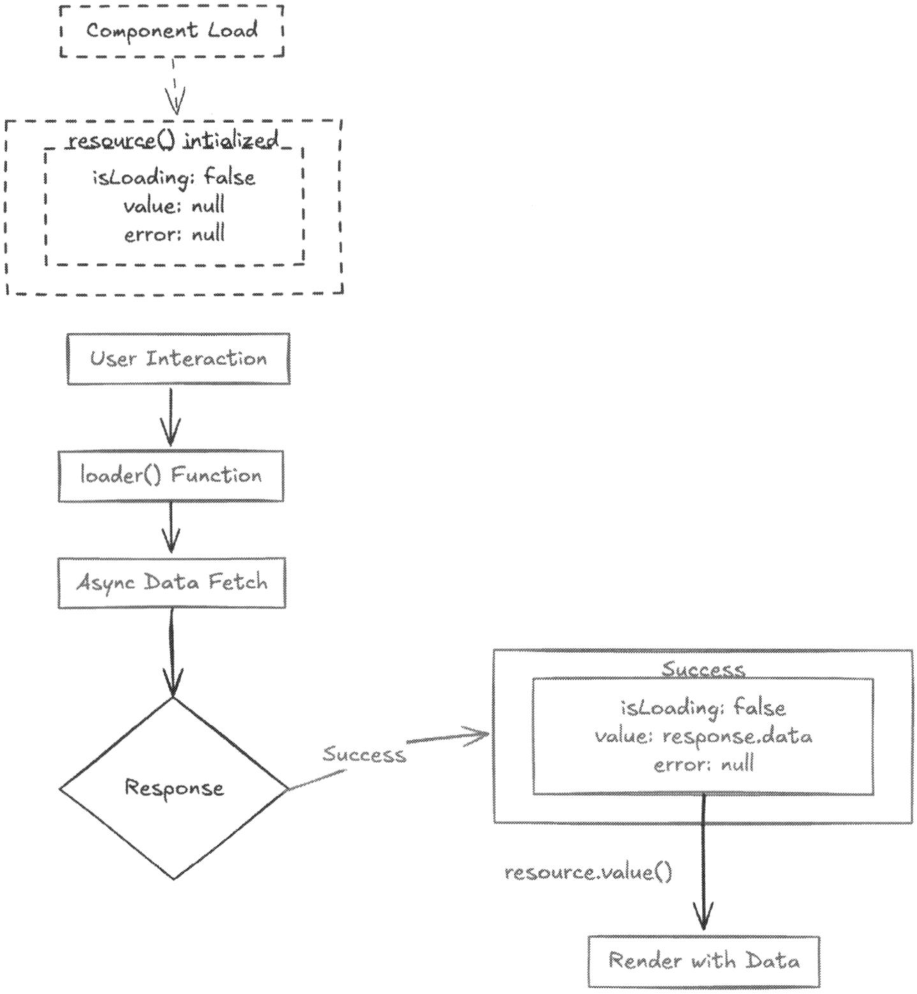

Figure 5.2 - loading *resource* on demand, when we have user interaction

Using the **`params`** method, we can control when the data is loaded and can make sure that a data fetch happens only when required. The key here is to return undefined from the **`resource`** when we don't want the resource to trigger the **`loader`** function at all.

Handling Errors

Data fetching isn't always smooth, so it's important to handle potential errors gracefully. Let's extend the application to include *error handling*, and to ***simulate*** an error when fetching the data.

We'll add a new button that attempts to fetch data with an error. This will demonstrate how to display error messages.

Here's the modified code:

```
import { Component, resource, signal } from '@angular/core';
interface WeatherData {
  temperature: number;
  condition: string;
  icon: string;
}

type WeatherRequestState = 'idle' | 'ready' | 'simulateError';

@Component({
  selector: 'app-weather-info',
  template: `
    <div class="card bg-base-200 w-96 shadow-xl mx-auto">
      <div class="card-body flex flex-col items-center gap-4">
        <button class="btn btn-block btn-primary btn-outline"
(click)="getWeatherInfo()">
          Fetch Weather
        </button>
        <button
          class="btn btn-block btn-error btn-outline"
          (click)="getWeatherInfoWithError()"
        >
          Get Weather Info with error
        </button>
        @if (weatherResource.isLoading()) {
          <span class="loading loading-spinner loading-lg"></span>
        } @else if (weatherResource.error()) {
          <div role="alert" class="alert alert-error">
            <svg>...</svg>
            <span>{{ weatherResource.error() }}</span>
          </div>
        } @else if (weatherResource.value()) {
          <img
            [src]="weatherResource.value()?.icon"
            class="w-20 object-fit"
            alt="weather icon"
          />
```

```
        <p class="text-2xl">
          Temperature: {{ weatherResource.value()?.temperature }}
        </p>
        <p class="text-xl">
          Condition: {{ weatherResource.value()?.condition }}
        </p>
      }
    </div>
  </div>
  `,
})
export class WeatherInfoComponent {
  weatherRequestState = signal<WeatherRequestState>('idle');
  weatherResource = resource<WeatherData, WeatherRequestState |
undefined>({
    params: () => {
      if (this.weatherRequestState() === 'idle') {
        return undefined;
      }
      return this.weatherRequestState();
    },
    loader: async ({ abortSignal, params: requestState }) => {
      const response = await new Promise<Response>((resolve) => {
        setTimeout(() => {
          fetch('assets/weather.json', { signal: abortSignal
}).then((r) =>
            resolve(r)
          );
        }, 1500);
      });
      if (!response.ok) {
        throw new Error('Could not fetch data');
      }
      if (requestState === 'simulateError') {
        throw new Error('Something went wrong');
      }
      const data = await response.json();
      return data as WeatherData;
    },
  });
```

```
  getWeatherInfo() {
    if (this.weatherRequestState() !== 'ready') {
      this.weatherRequestState.set('ready');
    } else {
      this.weatherResource.reload();
    }
  }

  getWeatherInfoWithError() {
    this.weatherRequestState.set('simulateError');
  }
}
```

In this example, we are showcasing how to display error messages using the **`resource`** method.

- We've added a **`simulateError`** state to the **`WeatherRequestState`** type.
- The **`weatherRequestState`** signal is now used to control if the loader should simulate an error.
- The **`loader`** function now checks if the request state is **`'simulateError'`**, and if it is, it throws a new error.
- The **`getWeatherInfoWithError()`** method sets the **`weatherRequestState`** to **`simulateError`**, triggering a data fetch with a simulated error.
- The **`template`** is updated to display the error using **`weatherResource.error()`**.

You can find the code of this example at **`` `apps/chapter-05/src/app/weather-info-with-error` ``**. From the code repository root, run the following command to serve the project:

```
nx serve chapter-05
```

Then, navigate to ***http://localhost:4200/weather-info-with-error*** to see the example

Figure 5.3 shows the process of how we handle errors with resources:

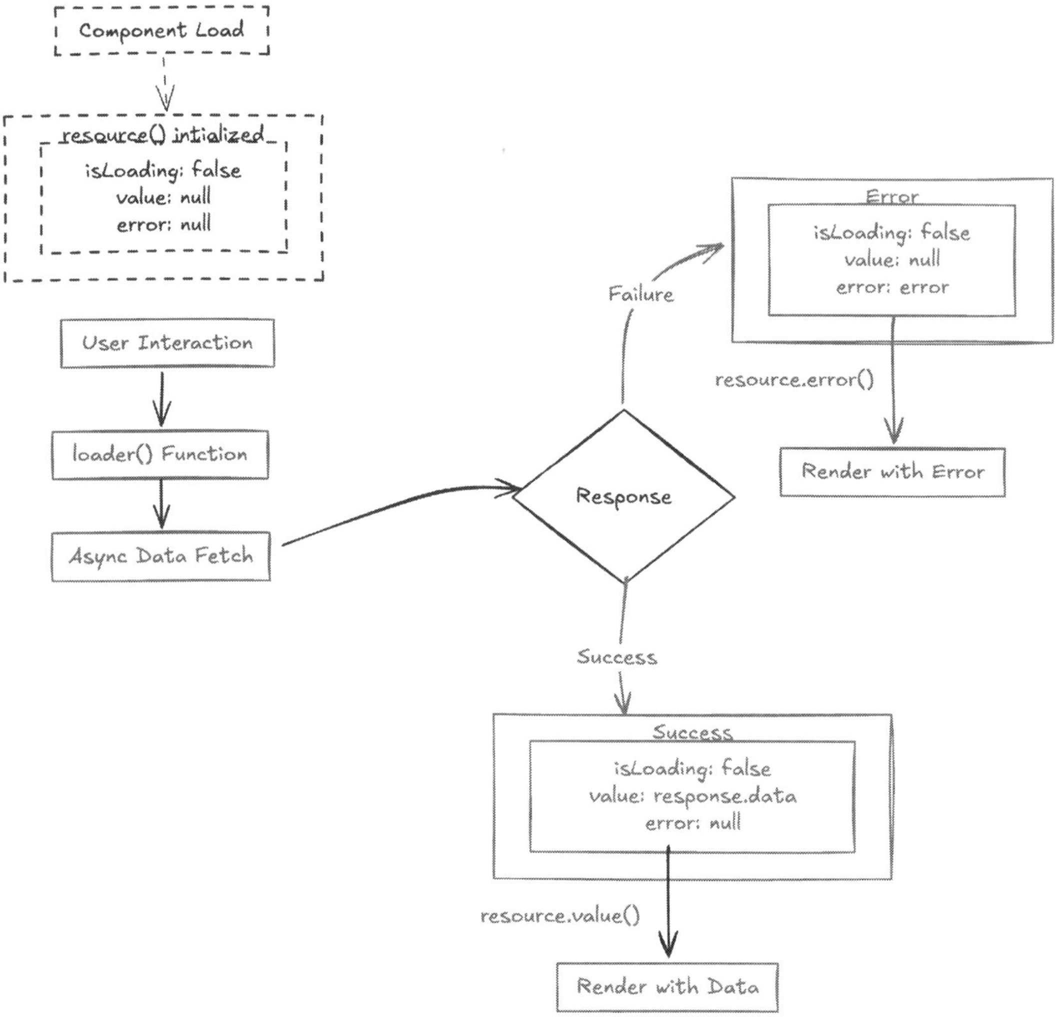

Figure 5.3 - handling errors with *resource*

By catching the errors in the loader function and using the **`error()`** state provided by the **`resource()`** method, we can gracefully manage errors in our components.

Dynamic Resource Switching (Multi-City Support)

Let's now introduce more ***dynamic*** behavior into our component by enabling the user to switch between ***single*** and ***multi-city*** modes. When switching modes, we'll modify how the resource fetches the data, using the **`params`** option to control the fetching process.

We'll be using different API calls for these two different modes. We'll add a toggle switch and a dropdown to allow the user to select their desired city when in ***multi-city*** mode.

Here's the complete component code:

```
import { Component, resource, signal } from '@angular/core';
import { FormsModule } from '@angular/forms';

type City = 'Stockholm' | 'Milan';

interface WeatherData {
  temperature: number;
  condition: string;
  icon: string;
  city?: City;
}

type WeatherRequestState = 'idle' | 'ready' | 'simulateError';

type WeatherResourceConfig = {
  requestState: WeatherRequestState;
  isMultiCityMode: boolean;
  selectedCity: City;
};

@Component({
  selector: 'app-weather-info',
  imports: [FormsModule],
  template: `
    <div class="card bg-base-200 w-96 shadow-xl mx-auto">
      <div class="card-body flex flex-col items-center gap-4">
        <div class="form-control w-full">
          <label class="label cursor-pointer">
            <span class="label-text">Multicity</span>
            <input
              (ngModelChange)="getWeatherInfo()"
              [(ngModel)]="isMultiCityMode"
              type="checkbox"
              class="toggle toggle-primary"
            />
          </label>
```

```
        </div>
        @if (isMultiCityMode()) {
          <select [(ngModel)]="selectedCity" class="select
select-primary w-full">
            @for(city of cities; track city) {
            <option [value]="city">{{ city }}</option>
            }
          </select>
        } @else {
          <button
            class="btn btn-block btn-primary btn-outline"
            (click)="getWeatherInfo()"
          >
            Get Weather Info
          </button>
        }
        <button
          class="btn btn-block btn-error btn-outline"
          (click)="getWeatherInfoWithError()"
        >
          Get Weather Info with error
        </button>
        @if (weatherResource.isLoading()) {
          <span class="loading loading-spinner loading-lg"></span>
        } @else if (weatherResource.error()) {
          <div role="alert" class="alert alert-error">
            <svg>...</svg>
            <span>{{ weatherResource.error() }}</span>
          </div>
        } @else if (weatherResource.value()) {
          <img
            [src]="weatherResource.value()?.icon"
            class="w-20 object-fit"
            alt="weather icon"
          />
          <p class="text-2xl">
            Temperature: {{ weatherResource.value()?.temperature }}
          </p>
          <p class="text-xl">
            Condition: {{ weatherResource.value()?.condition }}
          </p>
```

```
      }
    </div>
  </div>
  `,
})
export class WeatherInfoComponent {
  weatherRequestState = signal<WeatherRequestState>('idle');
  isMultiCityMode = signal<boolean>(false);
  cities: City[] = ['Stockholm', 'Milan'];
  selectedCity = signal<City>(this.cities[0]);
  weatherResource = resource<
    WeatherData | undefined,
    WeatherResourceConfig | undefined
  >({
    params: () => {
      if (this.weatherRequestState() === 'idle') {
        return undefined;
      }
      return {
        requestState: this.weatherRequestState(),
        isMultiCityMode: this.isMultiCityMode(),
        selectedCity: this.selectedCity(),
      };
    },
    loader: async ({ abortSignal, params }) => {
      if (!request) {
        return undefined;
      }
      const { requestState, isMultiCityMode, selectedCity } =
params;
      const response = await new Promise<Response>((resolve) => {
        setTimeout(() => {
          const url = isMultiCityMode
            ? 'assets/weather-multi.json'
            : 'assets/weather.json';
          fetch(url, { signal: abortSignal }).then((r) =>
resolve(r));
        }, 1500);
      });
      if (!response.ok) {
        throw new Error('Could not fetch data');
```

```
      }
      if (requestState === 'simulateError') {
        throw new Error('Something went wrong');
      }
      const data = await response.json();
      if (isMultiCityMode) {
        const weatherInfo = (data as WeatherData[]).find(
          (info) => info.city === selectedCity
        );
        if (!weatherInfo) {
          throw new Error('Weather info not found');
        }
        return weatherInfo;
      }
      return data as WeatherData;
    },
  });

  getWeatherInfo() {
    if (this.weatherRequestState() !== 'ready') {
      this.weatherRequestState.set('ready');
    } else {
      this.weatherResource.reload();
    }
  }

  getWeatherInfoWithError() {
    this.weatherRequestState.set('simulateError');
  }
}
```

In this example, we are dynamically switching between single and multi city modes, and handling the fetch behavior using the request method of the resource. The key takeaways are:

- We are controlling the resource **`loader`**, based on the **`weatherRequestState`** signal, initializing the resource on-demand.
- The **`params`** attribute is used to send more data to the loader.
- The loader now handles different scenarios: ***loading, errors, single city, and multi city***, using the value sent by the **`request`** attribute.

You can find the code of this example at `apps/chapter-05/src/app/weather-info-multiple-cities`. From the code repository root, run the following command to serve the project:

```
nx serve chapter-05
```

Then, navigate to ***http://localhost:4200/weather-info-multi-city*** to see the example

Figure 5.4 shows the process of using the two different modes for having a dynamic resource with different API calls:

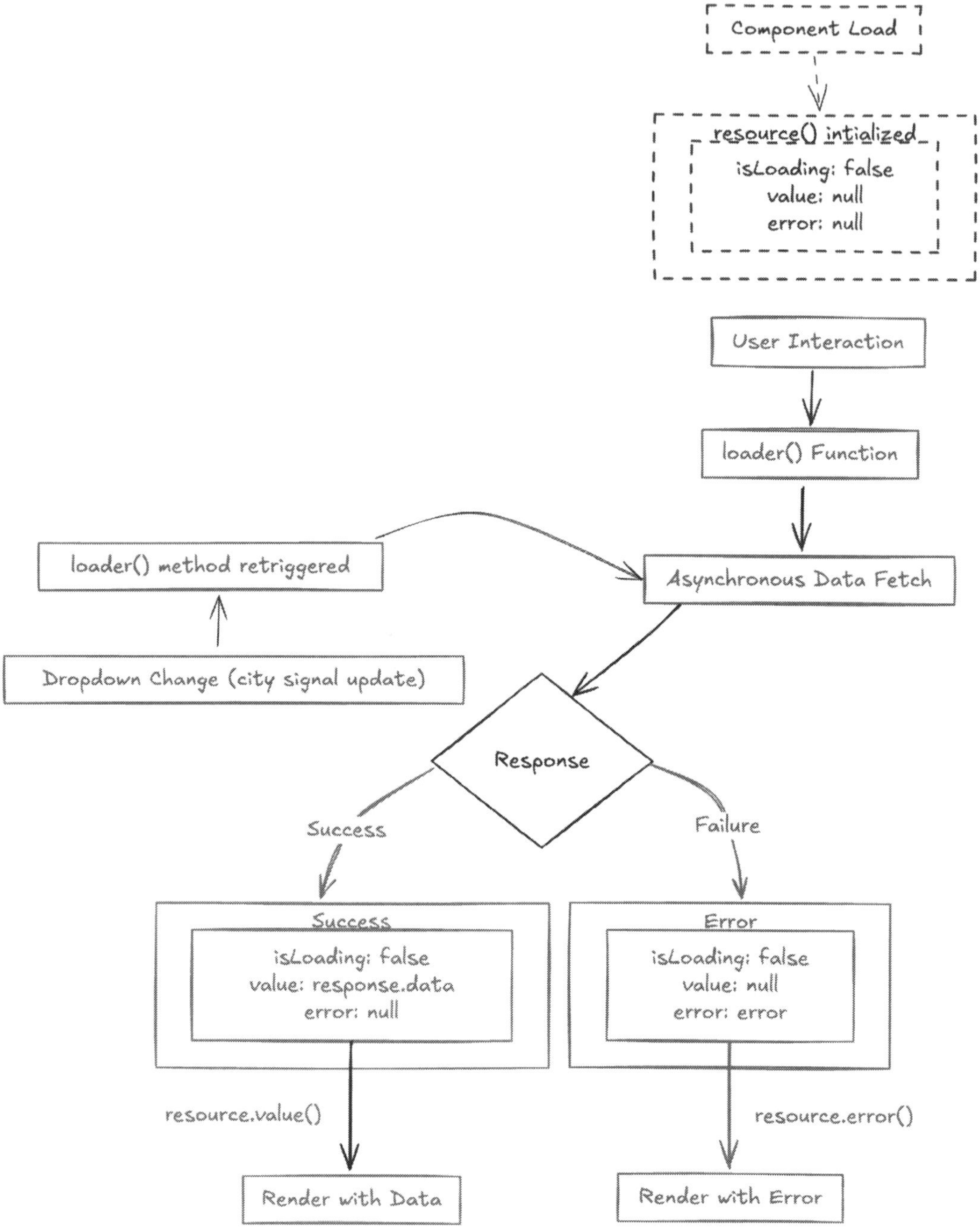

Figure 5.4 - dynamic resource trigger based on selected mode

Introducing `httpResource`: Simplified HTTP Data Fetching with Signals

Angular provides a specialized httpResource utility directly within @angular/common/http for streamlined integration of HttpClient operations with the Signals reactivity model. This utility offers a concise way to define a reactive data source based on HTTP requests, automatically managing loading, error, and success states, and making them available as signals.

This version of httpResource takes a loader function as its first argument. This loader function is responsible for returning the information needed to make the HTTP request, which can be as simple as a URL string or a more detailed HttpRequest object. A crucial feature is that this loader function can read other signals from your component. When these dependency signals change, calling the reload() method on the httpResource instance will re-evaluate the loader function, thus re-fetching data with the updated parameters.

Optionally, httpResource can take a second argument: an options object. This object can include a powerful parse function to transform the raw HTTP response or to implement custom error handling logic before httpResource sets its value or error signals.

Prerequisites:

- Ensure you have `provideHttpClient()` configured in your application (e.g., in `app.config.ts` or `main.ts`). This allows httpResource to use `HttpClient` internally.
- Import `httpResource` from `@angular/common/http`.
- Import `signal` from `@angular/core`.

Example: Dynamic Weather Data with httpResource (Single/Multi-City & Error Simulation)

```
import { httpResource } from '@angular/common/http';
import { Component, signal } from '@angular/core';
import { FormsModule } from '@angular/forms';

type City = 'Stockholm' | 'Milan';

interface WeatherData {
  temperature: number;
  condition: string;
  icon: string;
```

```
  city?: City;
}

type WeatherRequestState = 'idle' | 'ready' | 'simulateError';

@Component({
  selector: 'app-weather-info',
  imports: [FormsModule],
  template: `
    <!-- template is the same as the previous example -->
  `,
})
export class WeatherInfoComponent {
  weatherRequestState = signal<WeatherRequestState>('idle');
  isMultiCityMode = signal<boolean>(false);
  cities: City[] = ['Stockholm', 'Milan'];
  selectedCity = signal<City>(this.cities[0]);
  weatherResource = httpResource<WeatherData>(
    () => {
      const isMultiCityMode = this.isMultiCityMode();
      this.selectedCity();
      const url = isMultiCityMode
        ? 'assets/weather-multi.json'
        : 'assets/weather.json';
      return url;
    },
    {
      parse: (response) => {
        if (this.weatherRequestState() === 'simulateError') {
          this.weatherRequestState.set('idle');
          throw new Error('Something went wrong');
        }
        if (this.isMultiCityMode()) {
          const weatherInfo = (response as WeatherData[]).find(
            (info) => info.city === this.selectedCity()
          );
          if (!weatherInfo) {
            throw new Error('Weather info not found');
          }
          return weatherInfo;
        }
```

```
        return response as WeatherData;
      },
    }
  );

  getWeatherInfo() {
    if (this.weatherRequestState() !== 'ready') {
      this.weatherRequestState.set('ready');
    }
    this.weatherResource.reload();
  }

  getWeatherInfoWithError() {
    this.weatherRequestState.set('simulateError');
    this.weatherResource.reload();
  }
}
```

In this example, we're doing exactly what we did in the previous example, i.e. we are dynamically switching between single and multi city modes, and handling the fetch behavior using the request method of the resource. The key differences are:

- **Dynamic URL in Loader:** The first argument to `httpResource` is a loader function. This function reads component signals (`this.isMultiCityMode()` and `this.selectedCity()`) to determine which URL to return for the HTTP request.
- **`parse` Function for Transformation and Error Handling:**
    - The parse function (in the optional second options argument) receives the raw HTTP response.
    - It allows you to transform this response before it becomes the `value()` of the `httpResource`. In this example, if `isMultiCityMode` is true, it filters an array to find the data for the `selectedCity()`.
    - It can also be used to throw custom errors. Here, it checks `this.weatherRequestState()` to simulate an error if desired. Any error thrown here is caught by httpResource and made available via its `error()` signal.
- **.reload() Method for Re-fetching:**
    - The `weatherResource` instance has a `.reload()` method.

    - Calling `this.weatherResource.reload()` tells `httpResource` to re-execute its `loader` function. The loader will use the current values of `isMultiCityMode()` and `selectedCity()` to construct the new request, effectively refreshing the data or fetching data for a new selection.
- **Signal-Driven State:** The entire process is driven by signals. Component state signals (`isMultiCityMode`, `selectedCity`, `weatherRequestState`) influence the HTTP request and parsing, and the `httpResource` itself provides signals for `state()`, `isLoading()`, `value()`, and `error()` for reactive UI updates.
- Implicit `HttpClient`: Notice the component doesn't inject or directly use HttpClient. `httpResource` (from `@angular/common/http` and enabled by `provideHttpClient()`) handles the underlying HTTP mechanics.

> You can find the code of this example at `` `apps/chapter-05/src/app/weather-info-http-resource` ``. From the code repository root, run the following command to serve the project:
>
> ```
> nx serve chapter-05
> ```
>
> Then, navigate to ***http://localhost:4200/weather-info-http-resource*** to see the example

This example clearly demonstrates a clean and modern approach to handling dynamic HTTP requests with Angular Signals, using the `httpResource()` API. It showcases how component state signals can elegantly drive data fetching and how httpResource simplifies managing the reactive life cycle of these requests.

Conclusion

This progressive guide has demonstrated how to utilize Angular's `resource()` method for fetching data, handling errors, and dynamically switching between different fetching behaviors. By gradually building upon basic examples, we've explored how to manage diverse scenarios and how to control the initial loading of resources on-demand. We've also seen how to use the `params` attribute to send more information to the loader, adding flexibility to our data fetching process.

Chapter 6: Signal-Driven Components and Services

Introduction

Angular's new signal-based APIs revolutionize how components and services manage state, interact with the DOM, and communicate with each other. In this chapter, we'll explore `input()`, `output()`, `model()`, `viewChild()`, and other APIs through practical, real-world examples. You'll learn to build reactive UIs, share state across components, and integrate signals seamlessly with Angular's lifecycle. Let's dive into a shopping cart, a notification panel, and a dynamic form to see these APIs in action.

Signals in Components

Reactive Inputs with input()

Use `input()` to declare component inputs with built-in reactivity. Add **transforms** for **type coercion** or validation:

```
@Component({
  selector: 'app-user-card',
  template: `
    <div class="card">
      <h2>{{ userName() }}</h2>
      <p>Joined: {{ joinDate() | date }}</p>
    </div>
  `,
})
export class UserCardComponent {
  // Transform string input to uppercase
  userName = input('', {
    transform: (value: string) => value.toUpperCase()
  });

  // Transform date input (string | Date) to Date object always
  joinDate = input(new Date(), {
    transform: (value: string | Date) =>
```

```
      typeof value === 'string' ? new Date(value) : value
  });
}
```

Event Emission with output()

Emit events to parent components using output():

```
@Component({
  selector: 'app-notification-panel',
  template: `
    <div class="panel">
      <button (click)="markAllRead.emit()">Mark All Read</button>
    </div>
  `,
})
export class NotificationPanelComponent {
  markAllRead = output<void>(); // Emits void event
  notificationClicked = output<number>(); // Emits notification ID
}
```

Two-Way Binding with model()

Simplify two-way binding in forms or custom components:

```
@Component({
  selector: 'app-search',
  template: `
    <input
      [value]="query()"
      (input)="query.set($event.target.value)"
      placeholder="Search..."
    >
  `,
})
export class SearchComponent {
  query = model(''); // Parent binds with [(query)]="searchTerm"
}
```

Local State Management

Manage internal state with signals and update it functionally:

```
@Component({
  selector: 'app-counter',
  template: `
    <button (click)="decrement()">-</button>
    <span>{{ count() }}</span>
    <button (click)="increment()">+</button>
  `,
})
export class CounterComponent {
  count = signal(0);

  increment() {
    this.count.update(v => v + 1);
  }

  decrement() {
    this.count.update(v => Math.max(0, v - 1));
  }
}
```

Lifecycle Integration with effect()

Sync state with the DOM or external systems:

```
effect(() => {
  // Log count changes and update DOM attribute
  console.log('Current count:', this.count());
  this.hostElement.nativeElement.setAttribute('data-count',
this.count());
});
```

Component Communication

Parent-to-Child with input()

Pass reactive state from parent to child:

```
// Parent Component
@Component({
  template: `
    <app-notification-panel
[notifications]="alerts()"></app-notification-panel>
  `,
})
export class ParentComponent {
  alerts = signal<Notification[]>([]);
}
```

```
// Child Component
@Component({...})
export class NotificationPanelComponent {
  notifications = input<Notification[]>([]);
}
```

Child-to-Parent with output()

Emit events to parents:

```
// Child
@Component({
  template: `
    <div *ngFor="let notification of notifications()">
      <button (click)="notificationClicked.emit(notification.id)">
        {{ notification.text }}
      </button>
    </div>
  `,
})
export class NotificationPanelComponent {
  notifications = input<Notification[]>([]);
```

```
  notificationClicked = output<number>();
}
```

```
// Parent
@Component({
  template: `
    <app-notification-panel
      [notifications]="alerts()"
      (notificationClicked)="handleClick($event)"
    ></app-notification-panel>
  `,
})
export class ParentComponent {
  handleClick(notificationId: number) {
    // Mark notification as read
  }
}
```

Signals in Services

Shared State Management

Create a service to manage cart state across components:

```
@Injectable({ providedIn: 'root' })
export class CartService {
  private _items = signal<CartItem[]>([]);
  items = this._items.asReadonly(); // Expose readonly state

  addItem(item: CartItem) {
    this._items.update(items => [...items, item]);
  }

  removeItem(itemId: string) {
    this._items.update(items => items.filter(i => i.id !==
itemId));
  }
}
```

Service Lifecycle with effect()

Persist cart state to localStorage:

```
constructor() {
  // Load initial state
  const savedItems = localStorage.getItem('cart');
  if (savedItems) this._items.set(JSON.parse(savedItems));

  // Auto-save on changes
  effect(() => {
    localStorage.setItem('cart', JSON.stringify(this._items()));
  });
}
```

DOM Interactions with Signals

Dynamic Element Refs

Use **`viewChild`** and **`viewChildren`** to reference DOM elements:

```
@Component({
  template: `
    <button #submitButton>Submit</button>
    <ul>
      <li #listItems *ngFor="let item of items()">{{ item }}</li>
    </ul>
  `,
})
export class ListComponent {
  // Get a single element
  submitButton =
viewChild<ElementRef<HTMLButtonElement>>('submitButton');

  // Get a list of elements
  listItems = viewChildren<ElementRef>('listItems');

  ngAfterViewInit() {
    effect(() => {
      console.log('Submit button:',
```

```
this.submitButton()?.nativeElement);
    });
  }
}
```

Practical Example 1: Notifications Panel

Let's apply the signal-based APIs (`input()`, `output()`, `signal()`, `computed()`, `inject()`) to build a common application feature: a notification system. This example highlights a powerful **architectural pattern**: separating components into **smart** (or container) components and **presentational** (or dumb) components.

- Smart components are aware of services, manage application logic, fetch data, and prepare it for display.
- Presentational components receive data via inputs, display it, and emit user interaction events via outputs. They are unaware of the broader application context or services.

Our notification system will comprise three key parts:

- `NotificationsService`: The central authority for managing the notification state (the list of notifications and their read/unread status) using signals.
- `NotificationPanelComponent`: A reusable, presentational component (likely part of a UI library) responsible for displaying the notification bell icon, the count badge, and the list of notifications within a dropdown. It receives all data via inputs and emits an event when a user wants to mark a notification as read.
- `NotificationsPanelExampleComponent`: A smart component that consumes the `NotificationsService`, calculates necessary derived data (like the unread count), passes data down to the `NotificationPanelComponent`, and handles events coming up from it.

Notifications Service

The foundation is the `NotificationsService`, which holds the application state related to notifications.

```
// notification.service.ts
import { Injectable, signal } from '@angular/core';
import {
  DUMMY_NOTIFICATIONS,
  Notification,
} from '@modern-angular-signals-book/ui-lib'; // Domain types/data

// Singleton service available application-wide
@Injectable({ providedIn: 'root' })
export class NotificationsService {
  // --- State Signal ---
  // Private WritableSignal: Holds the source array of
notifications.
  // Initialized with dummy data for demonstration.
  private _notifications =
signal<Notification[]>(DUMMY_NOTIFICATIONS);

  // --- Public Signals ---
  // Public Readonly Signal: Exposes the notification list safely
to consumers.
  // Prevents direct mutation from outside the service.
  notifications = this._notifications.asReadonly();

  // --- Public Methods (State Changers) ---

  /**
   * Adds a new notification to the list immutably.
   * @param message The content of the notification.
   */
  addNotification(message: string) {
    // Use .update() to derive the next state based on the current
state,
    // ensuring immutability.
    this._notifications.update((currentNotifications) => [
      ...currentNotifications, // Keep existing notifications
      // Create and add the new notification object
      {
        id: crypto.randomUUID(), // Generate a unique ID
        message,
        read: false, // New notifications are initially unread
        title: 'New Notification',
```

```
        type: 'info',
        timestamp: new Date().toISOString(),
      },
    ]);
  }

  /**
   * Marks a specific notification as read based on its ID.
   * Updates the list immutably.
   * @param id The unique ID of the notification to mark as read.
   */
  markAsRead(id: string) {
    this._notifications.update((currentNotifications) =>
      // Use .map() to create a new array without modifying the
original objects directly,
      // except for the one being marked as read.
      currentNotifications.map(
        (notification) =>
          notification.id === id
            ? { ...notification, read: true } // Create a new
object with 'read' updated
            : notification // Return the original object if the ID
doesn't match
      )
    );
  }
}
```

Explanation:

- `@Injectable({ providedIn: 'root' })`: This makes our service a singleton available throughout the application.
- `private _notifications = signal<Notification[]>(DUMMY_NOTIFICATIONS)`: We initialize a private `WritableSignal` named `_notifications` with an array of notifications. This signal will hold the actual notification state. Keeping it `private` enforces encapsulation – only the service itself can directly write to this signal.
- `notifications = this._notifications.asReadonly()`: We expose a public notifications property. Instead of exposing the writable signal

directly, we use the `.asReadonly()` method. This creates a `Signal<Notification[]>` that components can read from but cannot directly modify using .set() or .update(). This is a crucial pattern for predictable state management.

- `addNotification(message: string)`: This method takes the notification text, generates a unique ID using `crypto.randomUUID()` (a modern browser API for generating UUIDs), sets the initial `read` status to `false`, and then uses the `.update()` method on `_notifications`. The `update` function receives the current array (`currentNotifications`), creates a new array containing all existing notifications (`...currentNotifications`) plus the new `notification` object, and returns this new array. This ensures ***immutability*** – we never modify the original array directly.
- `markAsRead(id: string)`: This method finds a notification by its id. It uses `.update()` and the array `.map()` method. `.map()` iterates over the `currentNotifications` and produces a new array. For each `notification`, it checks if the `id` matches the one passed in. If it matches, it creates a new notification object using the ***spread operator*** (`...notification`) but overrides the `read` property to `true`. If the id doesn't match, it returns the original `notification` object unchanged. This again ensures the update is ***immutable***.

With the service defined, components can now inject `NotificationsService` and read the notifications signal to display the list, while calling `addNotification` or `markAsRead` to interact with the state.

Notification Panel Component (Presentational)

Next, we'll look at the `NotificationPanelComponent` that consumes this service.

```
import { Component, computed, input, output } from '@angular/core';
import { NotificationItemComponent } from
'../notification-item/notification-item.component';
import { Notification } from '../../types/notification.type';

@Component({
  selector: 'lib-notification-panel',
  imports: [NotificationItemComponent],
  template: `
    <div class="dropdown dropdown-end">
      <button tabindex="0" role="button" class="btn btn-ghost
```

```
btn-circle">
        <div class="indicator">
          <svg>...</svg>

          <span class="...">{{
            count()
          }}</span>
        </div>
      </button>
      <div ...>
        <div ...>
          <div class="notification-panel">
            @for(notification of notifications(); track $index) {
            <lib-notification-item
              (click)="markAsRead.emit(notification.id)"
              [notification]="notification"
            />
            }
          </div>
        </div>
      </div>
    </div>
  `,
  styles: `...`,
})
export class NotificationPanelComponent {
  notifications = input.required<Notification[]>();
  notificationsCount = input.required<number>();
  count = computed(() => {
    if (this.notificationsCount() > 99) {
      return '+99';
    }
    return this.notificationsCount();
  });
  markAsRead = output<string>();
}
```

This component knows nothing about where the data comes from or what happens when **`markAsRead`** is emitted. It simply displays the **`notifications`** and **`notificationsCount`** it receives via signal inputs. It uses a **`computed()`**

signal for internal display logic (`count`). When a user clicks an item (handled within `lib-notification-item` or directly on it), it emits the notification's ID using the signal output, `markAsRead`.

NotificationsPanelExampleComponent (Smart Container)

This component connects the service (state management) and the panel (presentation).

```
import { Component, computed, inject } from '@angular/core';
import { NotificationPanelComponent } from
'@modern-angular-signals-book/ui-lib';
import { NotificationsService } from
'../services/notifications.service';

@Component({
  selector: 'app-notifications-panel-example',
  imports: [NotificationPanelComponent],
  template: `
    <div class="navbar bg-base-200 text-base-content p-4">
      <div class="flex-1">
        <a class="btn btn-ghost text-xl">Notifications panel
example</a>
      </div>
      <div class="flex-none">
        <lib-notification-panel
          [notifications]="notifications()"
          (markAsRead)="markNotificationsAsRead($event)"
          [notificationsCount]="unreadNotificationsCount()"
        />
      </div>
    </div>
  `,
  styles: ``,
})
export class NotificationsPanelExampleComponent {
  notificationsService = inject(NotificationsService);
  notifications = this.notificationsService.notifications;
  unreadNotificationsCount = computed(() => {
    return this.notifications().filter((noti) =>
!noti.read).length;
  });
```

```
  markNotificationsAsRead(id: string) {
    this.notificationsService.markAsRead(id);
  }
}
```

This smart component acts as the intermediary.

- It injects the `NotificationsService`.
- It reads the `notifications` signal from the service.
- It calculates the `unreadNotificationsCount` using a computed signal based on the service data.
- It passes the `notifications()` and `unreadNotificationsCount()` values down to the `lib-notification-panel` via `input` bindings (`[...]`).
- It listens for the `markAsRead` event coming up from the `lib-notification-panel` via `output` binding (`(...)`).
- When the event is received, its `handleMarkAsRead` method calls the appropriate method (`this.notificationService.markAsRead(id)`) on the service to update the application state.

This separation using smart and presentational components, facilitated by signal inputs and outputs, leads to a more modular, testable, and maintainable architecture. The presentational `NotificationPanelComponent` can be reused anywhere without needing the `NotificationsService`, while the `NotificationsPanelExampleComponent` encapsulates the specific logic for integrating the panel with the application's state management.

> You can find the code of this example at `` `apps/chapter-06/src/app/notifications-panel-example` ``. From the code repository root, run the following command to serve the project:
>
> `nx serve chapter-06`
>
> Then, navigate to ***http://localhost:4200/notifications-panel-example*** to see the example

Figure 6.1 shows how the components and the service work together:

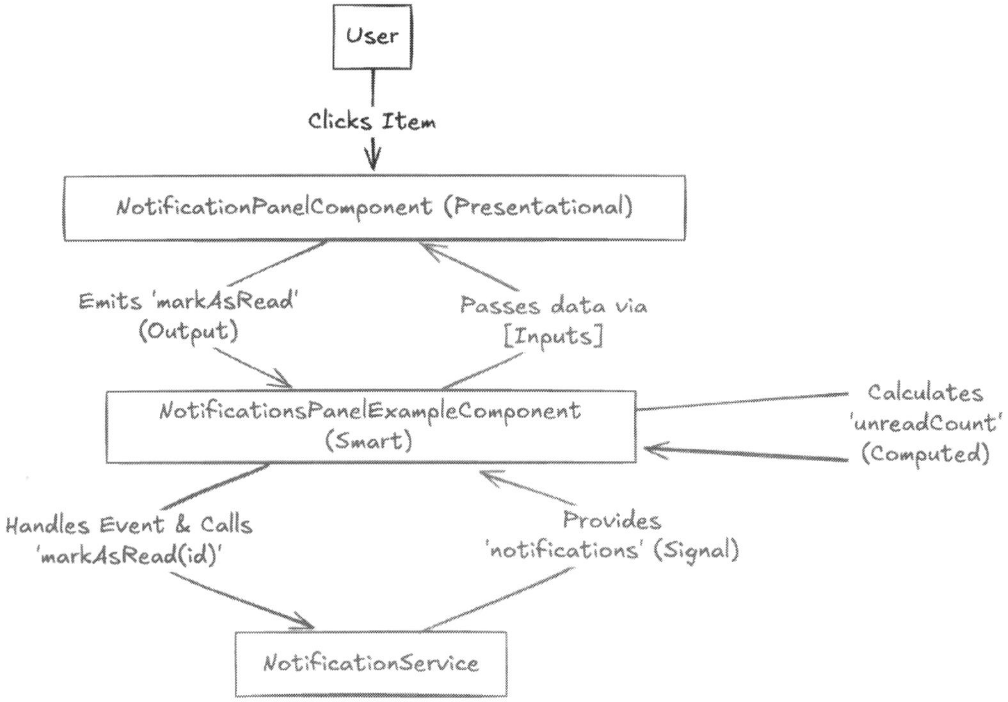

Figure 6.1 - NotificationsService, NotificationPanelComponent, and EventWithOutputsComponent working together

Practical Example 2: Shopping Cart

Our second example demonstrates how signals in a service can effectively manage shared state across different components. This example demonstrates managing shared state across multiple components using signals within a service. We will build a shopping cart feature that includes:

- Displaying a list of products.
- Adding products to a cart from the list.
- Searching/filtering the product list.
- Displaying a cart summary (item count, total price) in a persistent location (like a navbar).
- A dedicated view to show detailed cart contents with options to adjust quantity or remove items.

This example illustrates:

- **Shared State Management:** A `CartService` using signal and `computed` manages the cart's contents and derived totals.

- **Component Composition:** Using distinct presentational components for specific UI elements (`SearchBoxComponent`, `ProductsListComponent`).
- **Smart Container Components:** An `ShoppingCartExampleComponent` orchestrates the main product view and navbar summary, while a `CartComponent` manages the detailed cart view. Both interact with the CartService.
- **Two-Way Binding:** Using `model()` for the search input.
- **Effects for UI Feedback:** An effect triggers UI animations based on cart state changes.

Cart Service

The `CartService` centralizes the cart's state and logic. It manages the items in the cart and calculates totals reactively.

```
// cart.service.ts
import { Injectable, signal, computed } from '@angular/core';
import { Product } from '@ngneat/falso'; // Assuming Product type
is shared
import { CartItem } from '../types/cart.type';

@Injectable({ providedIn: 'root' }) // Global singleton service
export class CartService {
  // --- State ---
  // Private signal holding the array of CartItems. Initialized
empty.
  private _items = signal<CartItem[]>([]);

  // --- Selectors (Public Signals) ---
  // Read-only signal exposing the current cart items.
  items = this._items.asReadonly();

  // Computed signal that calculates the total price whenever items
change.
  totalPrice = computed(() =>
    this.items().reduce(
      (sum, item) => sum + Number(item.price) * item.quantity,
      0
    )
```

```
  );

  // Computed signal that calculates the total number of individual
items.
  itemCount = computed(() =>
    this.items().reduce((sum, item) => sum + item.quantity, 0)
  );

  // --- Actions (Public Methods) ---

  /** Adds a product to the cart or increments quantity if it
exists. */
  addItem(productToAdd: Product) {
    this._items.update((currentItems) => {
      const existingItemIndex = currentItems.findIndex(
        (item) => item.id === productToAdd.id
      );
      if (existingItemIndex > -1) {
        // Increment quantity immutably
        const updatedItems = [...currentItems];
        const currentItem = updatedItems[existingItemIndex];
        updatedItems[existingItemIndex] = {
          ...currentItem,
          quantity: currentItem.quantity + 1,
        };
        return updatedItems;
      } else {
        // Add as new item
        return [...currentItems, { ...productToAdd, quantity: 1 }];
      }
    });
  }

  /** Removes an item entirely from the cart by its ID. */
  removeItem(itemIdToRemove: string) {
    this._items.update(
      (currentItems) =>
        currentItems.filter((item) => item.id !== itemIdToRemove)
// Create new array excluding the item
    );
  }
```

```
  /** Updates the quantity of a specific item in the cart. Removes
if quantity < 1. */
  updateQuantity(itemId: string, newQuantity: number) {
    if (newQuantity < 1) {
      // Handle removal if quantity drops below 1
      this.removeItem(itemId);
      return;
    }
    this._items.update((currentItems) =>
      currentItems.map(
        (item) =>
          item.id === itemId ? { ...item, quantity: newQuantity } :
item // Update quantity immutably
      )
    );
  }

  /** Clears all items from the cart. */
  clearCart() {
    this._items.set([]); // Reset state to an empty array
  }
}
```

Role: This service is the single source of truth for the cart. Components inject it to access cart data (**`items`**, **`totalPrice`**, **`itemCount`**) and to modify the cart (**`addItem`**, **`removeItem`**, **`updateQuantity`**, **`clearCart`**).

Presentational Components

These components render UI based on inputs and emit events based on user actions.

Search Box (SearchBoxComponent)

```
// search-box.component.ts (ui-lib)
import { Component, model } from '@angular/core';
import { FormsModule } from '@angular/forms';

@Component({
```

```
  selector: 'lib-search-box',
  standalone: true,
  imports: [FormsModule],
  template: `
    <div class="form-control w-full flex gap-4 flex-col">
      <div class="join">
          <!-- Two-way binding via model() -->
        <input
          id="searchInput" type="text" placeholder="Search
products..."
          class="input input-bordered input-primary join-item
w-full focus:outline-none"
          [(ngModel)]="searchQuery"
        />
        <button class="btn btn-primary join-item"> <!-- Search Icon
-->
          <svg xmlns="http://www.w3.org/2000/svg" class="h-6 w-6"
fill="none" viewBox="0 0 24 24" stroke="currentColor"><path
stroke-linecap="round" stroke-linejoin="round" stroke-width="2"
d="M21 21l-6-6m2-5a7 7 0 11-14 0 7 7 0 0114 0z" /></svg>
        </button>
      </div>
    </div>
  `,
})
export class SearchBoxComponent {
  // Exposes a signal for two-way binding [(searchQuery)]
  searchQuery = model('');
}
```

Role: Provides a reusable search input. Uses `model()` for easy ***two-way binding*** with its parent.

Products List (ProductsListComponent)

```
// products-list.component.ts (ui-lib)
import { CurrencyPipe } from '@angular/common';
import { Component, input, output } from '@angular/core';
```

```
import { Product } from '@ngneat/falso';

@Component({
  selector: 'lib-products-list',
  imports: [CurrencyPipe],
  template: ` <div class="grid grid-cols-1 md:grid-cols-3 gap-4
mt-4">
    @for(product of products(); track product.id) {
    <!-- Use product.id for tracking -->
    <div class="card bg-base-200 shadow-xl">
      <figure class="px-4 pt-4">
        <img
          [src]="product.image"
          alt="{{ product.title }}"
          class="rounded-xl h-48 object-cover"
        />
      </figure>
      <div class="card-body">
        <h2 class="card-title">{{ product.title }}</h2>
        <p>{{ product.description }}</p>
        <div class="card-actions justify-between items-center
mt-4">
          <div class="text-xl font-bold">{{ product.price |
currency }}</div>
          <!-- Emit product object on button click -->
          <button class="btn btn-primary"
(click)="addToCart.emit(product)">
            Add to Cart
          </button>
        </div>
      </div>
    </div>
    } @empty {
    <p class="col-span-full text-center p-4">No products found.</p>
    <!-- Added empty state -->
    }
  </div>`,
  styles: ``,
})
export class ProductsListComponent {
  // Input: Receives the list of products to display. Required.
```

```
  products = input.required<Product[]>();
  // Output: Emits the Product object when the user wants to add
it.
  addToCart = output<Product>();
}
```

Role: Displays a grid of products. Receives the `products` array via a signal input and emits the specific `Product` object via the `addToCart` signal *output* when a button is clicked.

Main Smart Component (ShoppingCartExampleComponent)

This component integrates the search, product list, navbar cart summary, and the service.

```
// shopping-cart-example.component.ts
import { Component, computed, effect, inject, signal } from
'@angular/core';
import { RouterLink } from '@angular/router';
import { CurrencyPipe } from '@angular/common';
import { CartService, ProductsListComponent, SearchBoxComponent }
from '@modern-angular-signals-book/ui-lib';
import { Product, randProduct } from '@ngneat/falso';

@Component({
  selector: 'app-shopping-cart-example',
  imports: [SearchBoxComponent, ProductsListComponent, RouterLink,
CurrencyPipe],
  template: `
    <!-- Simplified Navbar -->
    <div class="navbar">
      <span>Shopping Example</span>
      <div class="cart-summary">
        <span>Items: {{ cartService.itemCount() }}</span> |
        <span>Total: {{ cartService.totalPrice() | currency
}}</span>
        <button routerLink="/cart">View Cart</button>
      </div>
    </div>
    <!-- Main Content -->
```

```
    <section class="p-2">
      <lib-search-box [(searchQuery)]="searchTerm" />
      <lib-products-list
        (addToCart)="addProductToCart($event)"
        [products]="filteredProducts()"
      />
    </section>
  `,
  styles: [`.navbar { display: flex; justify-content:
space-between; padding: 1rem; background: #eee; }`]
})
export class ShoppingCartExampleComponent {
  searchTerm = signal(''); // State for search
  cartService = inject(CartService); // Inject service

  // State for all products (ensure unique IDs)
  products = signal<Product[]>(randProduct({ length: 10 }).map(p =>
({...p, id: self.crypto.randomUUID()})));

  // Computed state for filtered products
  filteredProducts = computed(() => {
    const term = this.searchTerm().toLowerCase();
    if (!term) return this.products();
    return this.products().filter(p =>
p.title.toLowerCase().includes(term));
  });

  // Action handler: delegates to service
  addProductToCart(product: Product) {
    this.cartService.addItem(product);
  }

  // Effect can be added for simple logging or side effects if
needed
  constructor() {
    effect(() => {
      console.log('Cart item count changed:',
this.cartService.itemCount());
    });
  }
}
```

Role: This component acts as the main controller for the shopping view. It manages product data and search state locally using signals. It calculates `filteredProducts` using computed. It renders the `SearchBoxComponent` and `ProductsListComponent`, passing data down via inputs (`[products]`) and handling events up (`(addToCart)`). It also displays cart summary data (itemCount, totalPrice) directly from the CartService signals in its template's navbar section. The effect reacts to changes in `cartService.itemCount()` to trigger animations.

Cart View Component (CartComponent)

This component provides a dedicated page/view for the shopping cart details.

```
// cart.component.ts
import { CurrencyPipe, Location } from '@angular/common';
import { Component, inject } from '@angular/core';
import { CartService, CartItem } from
'@modern-angular-signals-book/ui-lib';

@Component({
  selector: 'app-cart',
  imports: [CurrencyPipe],
  template: `
    <button (click)="goBack()">Back</button>
    <div class="cart-view-simple">
      <h2>Cart Details</h2>
      @for(item of cartService.items(); track item.id) {
        <div class="cart-item-simple">
          <span>{{ item.title }} (Qty: {{ item.quantity }}) - {{
item.price * item.quantity | currency }}</span>
          <div> <!-- Basic controls -->
             <button (click)="decrementQuantity(item)">-</button>
             <input type="number" min="1" [value]="item.quantity"
(change)="updateCartQuantity(item, $event)" style="width: 40px;
text-align: center;">
             <button (click)="incrementQuantity(item)">+</button>
             <button (click)="cartService.removeItem(item.id)"
style="margin-left: 10px;">Remove</button>
          </div>
        </div>
```

```
    } @empty() { <p>Cart Empty</p> }

    @if(cartService.items().length > 0) {
      <div class="cart-total">
        <strong>Total: {{ cartService.totalPrice() | currency
}}</strong>
        <button (click)="checkout()">Checkout</button>
      </div>
    }
  </div>
  `
})
export class CartSimpleComponent {
  cartService = inject(CartService);
  location = inject(Location);

  updateCartQuantity(item: CartItem, event: Event) {
    const quantity = Number((event.target as
HTMLInputElement).value);
    this.cartService.updateQuantity(item.id, quantity);
  }
  incrementQuantity(item: CartItem) {
   this.cartService.updateQuantity(
     item.id, item.quantity + 1
   );
  }
  decrementQuantity(item: CartItem) {
    this.cartService.updateQuantity(
      item.id, item.quantity - 1
    );
  }
  goBack() { this.location.back(); }
  checkout() { alert('Checking out!');
this.cartService.clearCart(); }
}
```

Role: This component provides the dedicated cart management interface. It injects the `CartService` to read the items and `totalPrice` signals for display. User actions like changing quantity or removing items directly call methods on the **CartService**, ensuring the central state is updated.

> You can find the code of this example at `` `apps/chapter-06/src/app/shopping-cart-example` ``. From the code repository root, run the following command to serve the project:
>
> ```
> nx serve chapter-06
> ```
>
> Then, navigate to ***http://localhost:4200/shopping-cart-example*** to see the example

User flows

Let's discuss the user flows in the application to understand the example a bit better.

Search and Product Filtering Flow

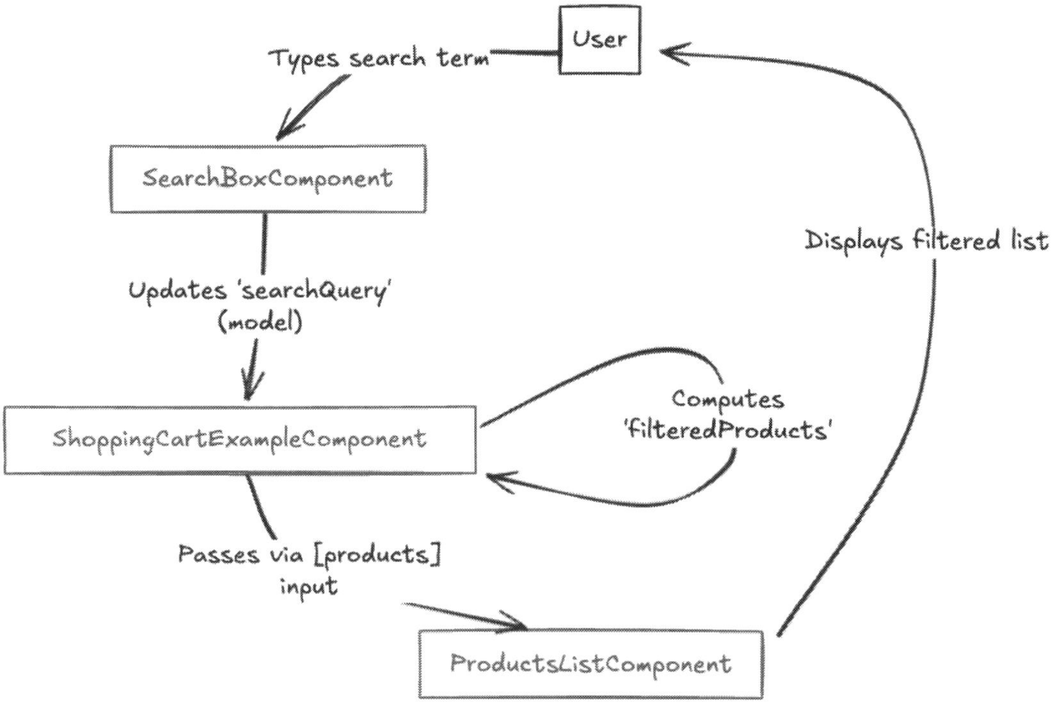

Figure 6.2 - User searches products via the SearchBoxComponent

The user interacts with the SearchBoxComponent. Thanks to the **model()** signal used for **searchQuery**, any change typed by the user is immediately reflected in the searchTerm signal within the

ShoppingCartExampleComponent (the smart component). This component then uses a computed signal (filteredProducts) which automatically re-evaluates whenever searchTerm (or the base products list) changes. The result of this computation (the filtered list) is passed down to the ProductsListComponent via its [products] input signal, causing it to re-render and display only the matching products to the user.

Adding an Item to the Cart Flow

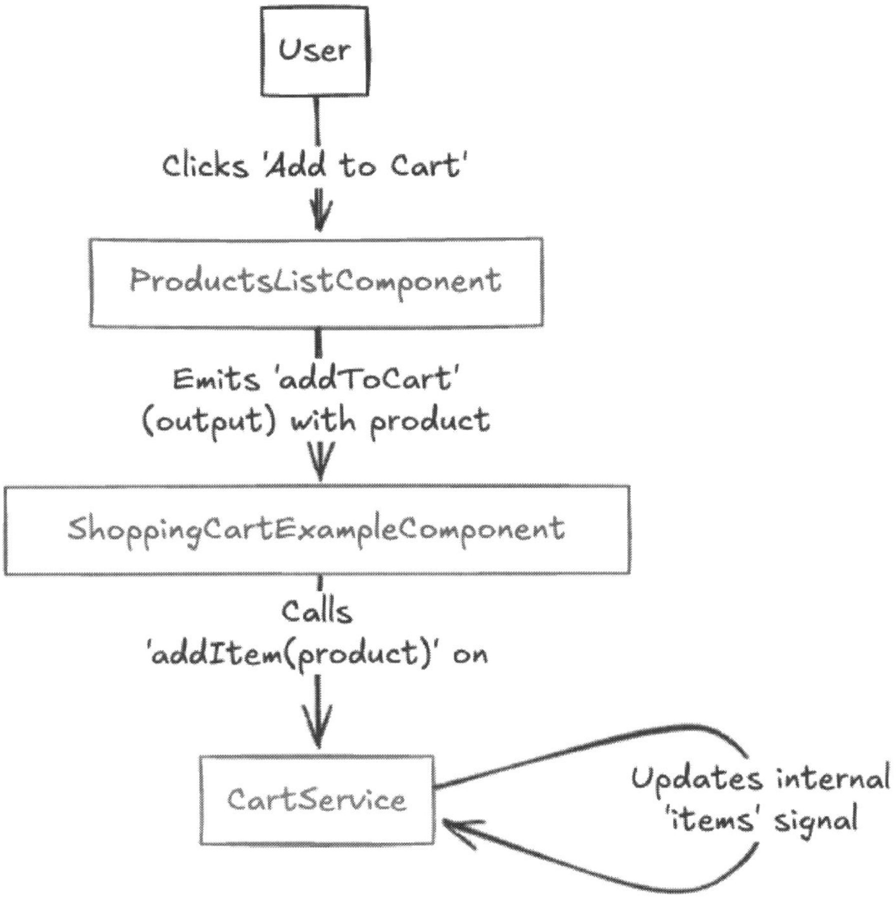

Figure 6.3 - User adding an item to cart

The user clicks the "Add to Cart" button within the ProductsListComponent. This component doesn't handle the logic itself; instead, it emits the specific Product object using its addToCart signal output. The parent ShoppingCartExampleComponent listens for this output event. Its event handler method (addProductToCart) then takes the received Product and calls the addItem method on the injected CartService. The CartService updates its internal `_items` signal, which in turn causes any `computed` signals depending on it (like `itemCount` and `totalPrice`) to automatically update.

Displaying Cart Summary in Navbar Flow

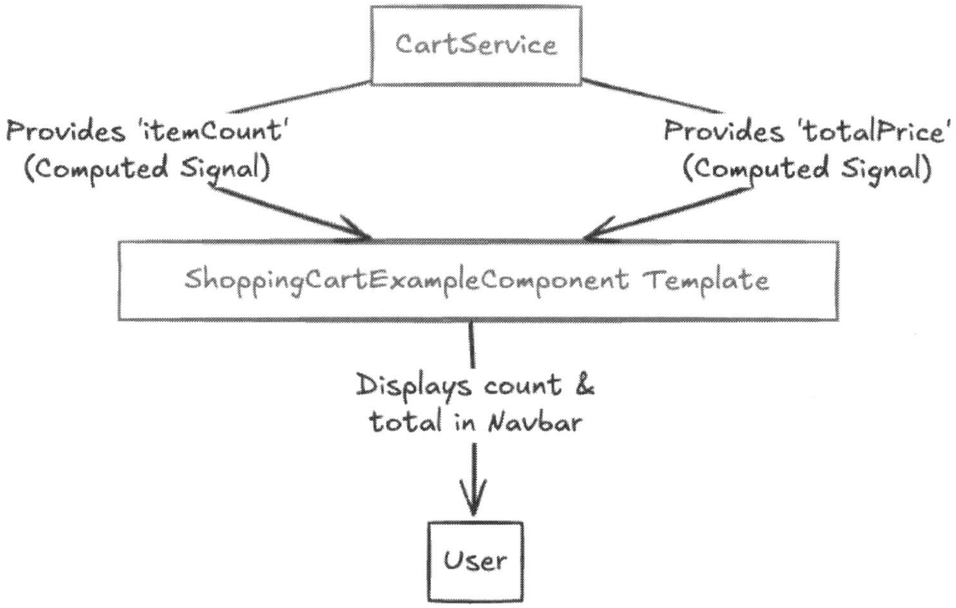

Figure 6.4 - Displaying cart summary in the Navbar

The `ShoppingCartExampleComponent` injects the `CartService`. Within its template (specifically the navbar section), it directly reads the computed signals `itemCount()` and `totalPrice()` from the service. Because these are signals derived from the cart's items state, the navbar display automatically updates whenever an item is added or removed via the service, without the `ShoppingCartExampleComponent` needing explicit refresh logic for the summary display. The effect in the component also reads `itemCount()` to trigger animations based on these changes.

Managing Items in the Cart View Flow

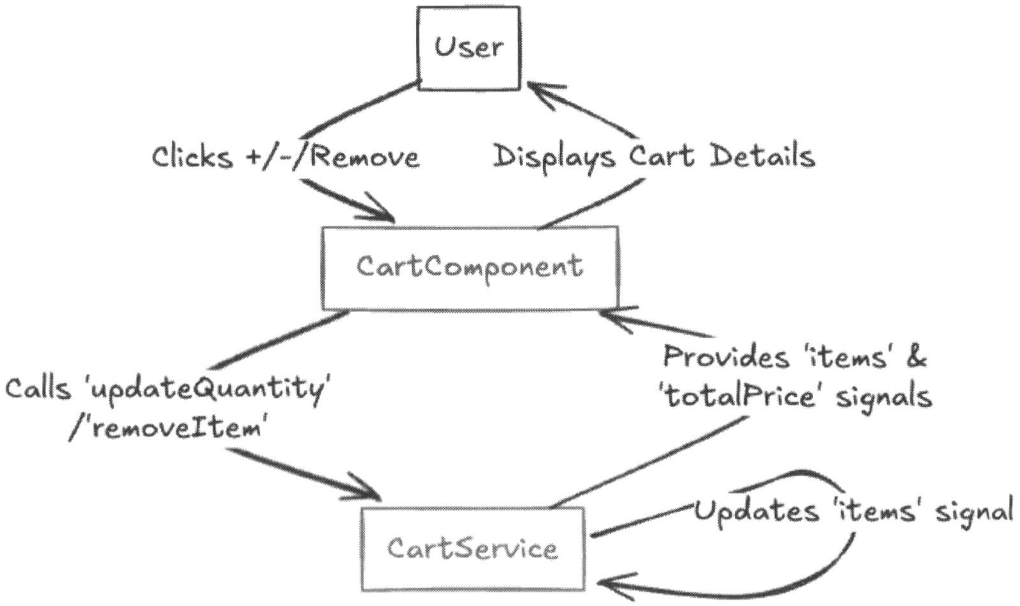

Figure 6.5 - User adding or removing the items from cart

The `CartComponent` (the dedicated cart view) directly injects and uses the `CartService`. For displaying the cart contents and the total, it reads the `items()` and `totalPrice()` signals within its template. When the user interacts with quantity buttons or the remove button within this view, the corresponding methods (`incrementQuantity`, `decrementQuantity`, `updateCartQuantity`, `removeItem`) in `CartComponent` are called. These methods, in turn, delegate the state update logic by calling the appropriate methods (`updateQuantity`, `removeItem`) on the `CartService`. This ensures that the central cart state is modified correctly, and all dependent signals (including those read by this component and the main `ShoppingCartExampleComponent`) update automatically.

Summary

This example showcases a slightly more complex application structure using signals. A central service manages the core state (`CartService`). Presentational components handle specific UI tasks (`SearchBoxComponent`, `ProductsListComponent`). Smart components (`ShoppingCartExampleComponent`, `CartComponent`) consume the service, derive necessary view state (like filtered products), orchestrate interactions between child components and the service, and sometimes manage local UI state (like `searchTerm` or animation triggers). This separation promotes modularity and leverages signals for reactive updates across the application.

Practical Example 3: Dynamic List with DOM Interaction

Signals offer powerful integration with the DOM through the `viewChild` (for single elements) and `viewChildren` (for multiple elements) query functions. These return signals whose values are `ElementRef`(s), updating automatically as elements are added, removed, or changed in the view. This allows for reactive interactions with template elements.

This example demonstrates a dynamic list component where:

- A list of items is managed using a signal and rendered with `@for`.
- `viewChild` obtains reactive references to the "Add Item" input and button.
- `viewChildren` obtains reactive references to the rendered list item (`<li>`) elements.
- An `effect` disables the submit button based on an `isProcessing` signal.
- A `computed` signal identifies newly added `<li>` elements.
- An `effect` uses the `computed` signal and `querySelector` to apply a temporary highlight animation to a div inside the newly added `<li>` elements.
- `afterNextRender` hook sets initial focus on the input field.

This example showcases:

- **Signal-based DOM Queries:** `viewChild` and `viewChildren` returning reactive `ElementRef` signals.
- **Reacting to Query Results:** Using `effect` and `computed` with the signal returned by `viewChildren`.
- **DOM Manipulation:** Modifying element properties (`disabled`) and accessing/modifying child elements (`querySelector`, `classList`) within effects.
- **Post-Render Logic:** Using `afterNextRender` for initial DOM setup.

Dynamic List Component (DynamicListComponent)

```
// dynamic-list.component.ts
import {
  Component,
  effect,
  viewChild, // For single element queries
  viewChildren, // For multiple element queries
  ElementRef, // Type for element references
  signal,
  afterNextRender, // Lifecycle hook for post-render actions
  computed,
} from '@angular/core';
import { FormsModule } from '@angular/forms'; // For
ngNativeValidate

@Component({
  selector: 'app-dynamic-list',
  standalone: true,
  imports: [FormsModule],
  template: `
    <div class="card bg-base-200 shadow-xl p-4 max-w-lg mx-auto">
      <!-- Form for adding items -->
      <form class="flex gap-2 mb-4" (submit)="addItem()"
ngNativeValidate>
        <!-- Query input with viewChild -->
        <input
          #newItemInput
          name="newItemInputVal"
          type="text"
          required
          class="input input-bordered flex-1"
          placeholder="Add new item"
        />
        <!-- Query button with viewChild -->
        <button #submitButton class="btn btn-primary"
type="submit">
          Add Item
        </button>
      </form>
```

```
      <!-- List rendering -->
      <ul class="menu bg-base-100 rounded-box gap-1">
        <!-- Query *inner divs* with viewChildren -->
        @for(item of items(); track item; let idx = $index) {
        <li #listItems [attr.data-item-value]="item">
          <!-- Outer list item -->
          <!-- Inner div contains content and is queried -->
          <div class="list-item-inner flex justify-between
items-center">
            <span>{{ item }}</span>
            <button
              class="btn btn-sm btn-ghost text-error"
              (click)="removeItem(idx)"
            >
              ×
            </button>
          </div>
        </li>
        } @empty {
        <li class="text-center text-gray-500 p-2">List is
empty.</li>
        }
      </ul>

      <!-- Item count display -->
      <div class="mt-4 text-sm text-gray-500">
        Total items: {{ items().length }}
      </div>
    </div>
  `,
  styles: [
    `
      /* Style applied to the inner div for highlighting */
      .list-item-inner.new-item-highlight {
        transition: background-color 0.5s ease-out;
        background-color: var(--color-primary);
        border-radius: var(--rounded-btn, 0.5rem);
        > * {
          color: var(--color-primary-content);
        }
      }
```

```
    `,
  ],
})
export class DynamicListComponent {
  // --- Signal-based element references ---
  submitButton =
viewChild<ElementRef<HTMLButtonElement>>('submitButton');
  // Signal for the list of *inner div* elements marked with
#listItems.
  listItems =
viewChildren<ElementRef<HTMLDivElement>>('listItems'); // Querying
DIVs now
  newItemInput =
viewChild<ElementRef<HTMLInputElement>>('newItemInput');

  // --- Component state signals ---
  items = signal<string[]>(['Initial Item 1', 'Initial Item 2']);
  isProcessing = signal(false); // Example state for button disable

  // --- Computed signal for animation ---
  // Finds *inner div* elements that haven't been animated.
  itemsToAnimate = computed(() =>
    this.listItems().filter(
      (elRef) => !elRef.nativeElement.hasAttribute('data-animated')
    )
  );

  constructor() {
    // --- Effects ---

    // Effect 1: Manage submit button's disabled state.
    effect(() => {
      const buttonRef = this.submitButton();
      if (buttonRef) {
        buttonRef.nativeElement.disabled = this.isProcessing();
      }
    });

    // Effect 2: Highlight newly added list item divs.
    effect(() => {
      const newlyAddedDivRefs = this.itemsToAnimate(); // Get refs
```

```
to new inner divs
      console.log('New list item divs detected:',
newlyAddedDivRefs.length);

      if (newlyAddedDivRefs.length > 0) {
        // Apply highlight class to the inner divs
        newlyAddedDivRefs.forEach((elRef) => {
          const innerDiv =
            elRef.nativeElement.querySelector('.list-item-inner');
          if (innerDiv) {
            innerDiv.classList.add('new-item-highlight');
          }
          // Mark as processed
          elRef.nativeElement.setAttribute('data-animated',
'true');
        });

        // Remove highlight after a short delay
        setTimeout(() => {
          newlyAddedDivRefs.forEach((elRef) => {
            const innerDiv =

elRef.nativeElement.querySelector('.list-item-inner');
            if (innerDiv) {
              innerDiv.classList.remove('new-item-highlight');
            }
          });
        }, 500);
      }
    });

    // --- Lifecycle Hooks ---
    // Set focus on the input after the initial render.
    afterNextRender(() => {
      this.newItemInput()?.nativeElement.focus();
    });
  }

  // --- Component Methods ---
  addItem() {
    const inputElement = this.newItemInput()?.nativeElement;
```

```
    if (!inputElement?.value) return;
    // this.isProcessing.set(true); // Simulate processing if
needed
    this.items.update((currentItems) => [...currentItems,
inputElement.value]);
    inputElement.value = '';
    inputElement.focus();
    // setTimeout(() => this.isProcessing.set(false), 300);
  }

  removeItem(indexToRemove: number) {
    this.items.update((currentItems) =>
      currentItems.filter((_, index) => index !== indexToRemove)
    );
  }
}
```

Let's dissect the code a bit:

- `viewChild` & `viewChildren`: These functions query elements using template reference variables (`#...`). `viewChild` is used for single elements (`#newItemInput`, `#submitButton`), returning a `Signal<ElementRef | undefined>`. `viewChildren('listItems')` targets all `<li>` elements with `#listItems`, returning a `Signal<ReadonlyArray<ElementRef<HTMLLIElement>>>`.
- **Reading Query Signals:** Within effects or other component logic, reading the signal (e.g., `this.listItems()`) provides the current `ElementRef`(s).
- **Reacting to Queries:**
  - An effect reads `submitButton()` and `isProcessing()` to control the button's `disabled` state.
  - The `itemsToAnimate` computed signal reads `listItems()` and filters the array of `<li>` ElementRefs based on a data-animated attribute check.
  - The animation effect reads `itemsToAnimate()`. For each new `<li>` `ElementRef`, it uses `liRef.nativeElement.querySelector('.list-item-inner')` to find the nested `div` and applies the highlight class to it. It marks the parent `<li>` with `data-animated` to prevent re-animation.

- **afterNextRender:** This hook ensures the `newItemInput` element is available in the DOM before attempting to focus it.

In this example, we use Signal-based DOM queries (`viewChild`, `viewChildren`) to provide a reactive link between component logic and template elements. Effects and computed signals can directly consume these query signals, allowing for precise and declarative DOM interactions based on component state or the presence/absence of elements themselves.

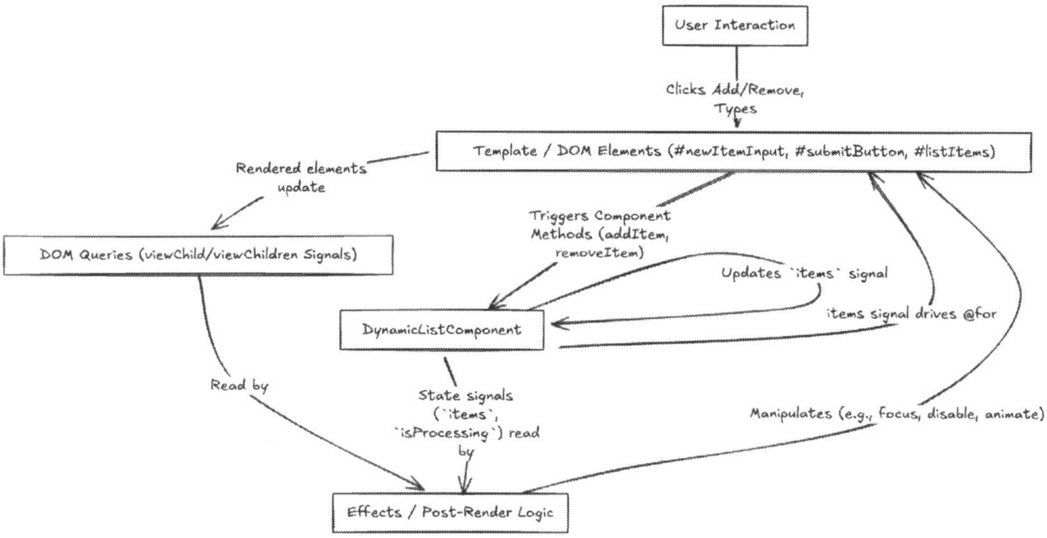

Figure 6.6 - User interactions with Signal APIs for the Dynamic List & DOM interaction

> You can find the code of this example at `apps/chapter-06/src/app/dynamic-list`. From the code repository root, run the following command to serve the project:
>
> ```
> nx serve chapter-06
> ```
>
> Then, navigate to ***http://localhost:4200/dynamic-list*** to see the example

Signal-based DOM queries (`viewChild`, `viewChildren`) provide a reactive link between component logic and template elements. Effects and computed signals can directly consume these query signals, allowing for precise and declarative DOM interactions based on component state or the presence/absence of elements themselves.

Conclusion

This chapter showcased the practical power and versatility of Angular Signals through several real-world examples. We've moved from foundational concepts to building interactive features like a notification panel, a multi-component shopping cart, a dynamic form with reactive validation, and a list interacting directly with the DOM via signal-based queries.

Key takeaways include:

- **Signal-based APIs (`input`, `output`, `model`, `viewChild`, `viewChildren`)** streamline component interactions, offering reactive and type-safe alternatives to traditional decorators.
- **Services as State Hubs:** Using `signal()` and `computed()` within services creates centralized, predictable, and easily consumable state management solutions.
- **Declarative Reactivity:** `computed()` signals excel at deriving state (like validation status, filtered lists, or calculated totals), automatically updating whenever their dependencies change.
- **Managed Side Effects:** `effect()` provides a dedicated place to interact with external systems (DOM, timers, logging, storage) in response to signal changes, complete with cleanup mechanisms.
- **Architectural Patterns:** Signals naturally encourage patterns like smart/presentational components, promoting modularity and testability.

By integrating these signal-based tools, you can build Angular applications that are often cleaner, more performant, easier to reason about, and better aligned with modern reactive programming principles.

The journey into signals often involves integrating with existing applications or libraries built with RxJS. Understanding how these two powerful reactive paradigms work together is essential for modern Angular development.

In the next chapter, we'll explore migrating existing RxJS-based apps to signals and combining both paradigms effectively.

Chapter 7: Interoperability and Migration Strategies

Introduction

As we journey deeper into the realm of Angular Signals, a crucial question arises for many seasoned Angular developers: how do Signals integrate with existing applications heavily reliant on RxJS? The Angular ecosystem has been built upon the robust foundation of RxJS for years, and numerous applications, libraries, and even developer habits are deeply intertwined with Observables. Fear not! Angular Signals are designed not to replace RxJS entirely, but to augment and enhance it. This chapter will serve as your guide to navigate this transition, outlining effective strategies for bridging the gap between Signals and Observables, enabling a gradual migration to a signal-based architecture, and ensuring your applications remain robust and maintainable throughout the process. We are entering the era of hybrid reactive applications, and understanding seamless interoperability is key to modern Angular mastery.

Signals and Observables: Bridging Reactivity

Angular provides two powerful utilities, `toSignal()` and `toObservable()`, within the `@angular/core/rxjs-interop` package, specifically designed to facilitate communication between the Signal and Observable worlds. Let's explore each in detail.

toSignal(): Converting Observables to Signals

Imagine you have an existing service that exposes data as an RxJS Observable. You want to leverage this data within your component's template or in a computed signal, enjoying the fine-grained reactivity of Signals. `toSignal()` is your bridge. This function converts an Observable into a *read-only* Signal, allowing you to consume Observable streams as reactive Signals.

Let's consider a practical example. Suppose you have a `UserDataService` that provides a stream of live user counts as an `Observable` (`liveUsersCount$`), and you want to use this in a Signal-based service (`UserToSignalService`) or component.

```
// user-data.service.ts (Simplified)
import { Injectable } from '@angular/core';
import { interval, map, Observable, shareReplay, startWith } from
```

```
'rxjs';

@Injectable({ providedIn: 'root' })
export class UserDataService {
  readonly liveUsersCount$: Observable<number> =
interval(1500).pipe(
    startWith(0),
    map(() => Math.floor(Math.random() * 1000)),
    shareReplay(1)
  );
  // ... other methods/properties
}

// user-to-signal.service.ts (Simplified - showcasing conversion)
import { computed, inject, Injectable, Signal } from
'@angular/core';
import { toSignal } from '@angular/core/rxjs-interop';
import { UserDataService } from './user-data.service';
import { UserStats } from '../interfaces'; // Assuming UserStats
interface exists

@Injectable({ providedIn: 'root' })
export class UserToSignalService {
  private userDataService = inject(UserDataService);

  // Convert Observable to Signal
  private readonly liveUsers: Signal<number> = toSignal(
    this.userDataService.liveUsersCount$.pipe(
      // catchError(() => of(0)) // Optionally handle errors
    ),
    { initialValue: 0 } // Provide an initial value
  );

  // Use the converted signal in computed signals
  private readonly peakUsers = computed(() => this.liveUsers() +
200);
  private readonly averageUsers = computed(() =>
Math.floor(this.liveUsers() * 0.8));
  // ... other computed signals

  readonly userStats: Signal<UserStats> = computed(() => ({
```

```
    count: this.liveUsers(),
    peak: this.peakUsers(),
    average: this.averageUsers(),
    // ...
  }));
}

// observables-to-signals.component.ts (Simplified - showcasing
usage)
import { Component, inject } from '@angular/core';
import { UserToSignalService } from
'../services/user-to-signal.service';
// ... imports for StatsComponent

@Component({
  selector: 'app-observables-to-signals-demo',
  template: `
    <!-- Template uses userStats() signal -->
    <app-stats [userStats]="userStats()" />
  `,
  // ... other component metadata
})
export class ObservablesToSignalsComponent {
  private userWSignalService = inject(UserToSignalService);
  protected readonly userStats = this.userWSignalService.userStats;
}
```

Explanation:

- **Import `toSignal`:** We import toSignal from `@angular/core/rxjs-interop`.
- **Inject `UserDataService`:** We inject our existing `UserDataService` that provides the `liveUsersCount$` Observable.
- **`toSignal()` Conversion:** In `UserToSignalService`, we use `toSignal()` to wrap the `userDataService.liveUsersCount$` Observable.
    - **First Argument:** The Observable we want to convert (`userDataService.liveUsersCount$`). You can chain RxJS operators like `catchError` here if needed before passing to toSignal.

    - **Second Argument (Optional):** We provide an options object with `initialValue: 0`. This is crucial because Observables are inherently asynchronous. `toSignal()` needs an initial value to return before the Observable emits its first value. This ensures your template or computed signals can work without errors during the initial loading phase.
- **Usage:** The resulting `liveUsers` is a read-only `Signal<number>`. We can now use it within `computed()` signals (`peakUsers`, `averageUsers`, `userStats`) just like any other Signal. The component (`ObservablesToSignalsComponent`) can then consume the final userStats signal directly in its template.

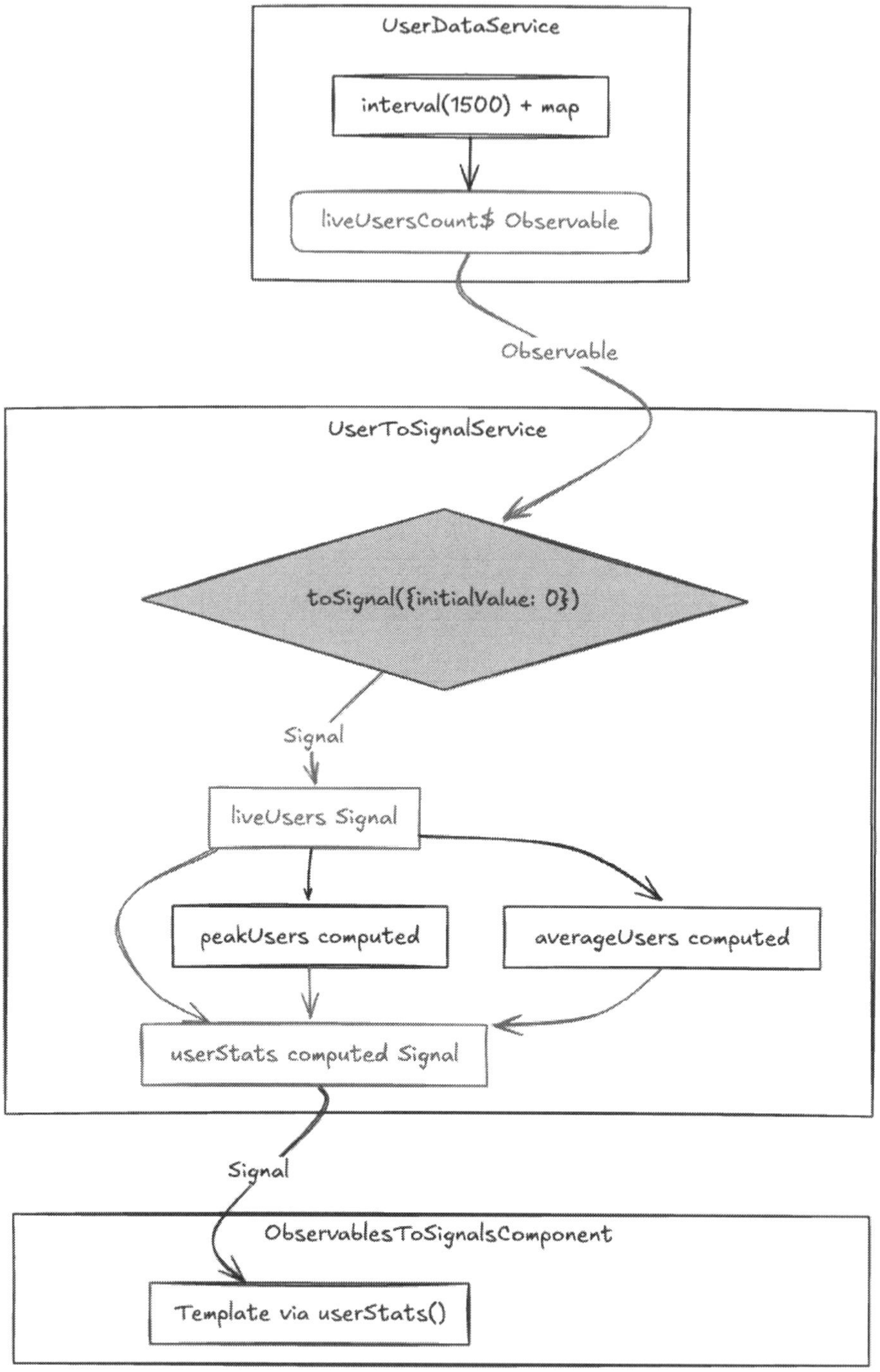

Figure 7.1 - Converting liveUsersCount$ observable to a signal using toSignal() method

You can find the code of this example at `**apps/chapter-07/src/app/observables-to-signals**`. From the code repository root, run the following command to serve the project:

```
nx serve chapter-07
```

Then, navigate to ***http://localhost:4200/obs-to-signals*** to see the example

toObservable(): Converting Signals to Observables

Conversely, you might have a Signal that you need to integrate with an RxJS-based service or utilize within RxJS operators. `toObservable()` provides the reverse bridge, converting a Signal into a cold Observable. This Observable will emit the Signal's current value upon subscription and subsequently emit whenever the Signal's value changes.

Let's imagine a `SensorService` that manages a `rawSensor` Signal and needs to expose processed versions of this data as Observables, perhaps for integration with other RxJS-based parts of the application or to leverage specific RxJS operators.

```
// sensor.service.ts (Simplified)
import { Injectable, signal } from '@angular/core';
import { toObservable } from '@angular/core/rxjs-interop';
import { Observable } from 'rxjs';
import { debounceTime, distinctUntilChanged, map } from
'rxjs/operators';

@Injectable({ providedIn: 'root' })
export class SensorService {
  // Base signal that updates with raw sensor data
  readonly rawSensor = signal(20); // Starting at 20°C

  private readings: number[] = [];

  readonly rawSensor$: Observable<number> =
toObservable(this.rawSensor);

  // Apply RxJS operators to the Observable derived from the Signal
  readonly stabilizedTemp$: Observable<number> =
this.rawSensor$.pipe(
```

```
      debounceTime(500),
      distinctUntilChanged()
  );

  readonly averageTemp$: Observable<number> = this.rawSensor$.pipe(
    map((current) => {
      this.readings.push(current);
      if (this.readings.length > 5) this.readings.shift();
      return this.readings.reduce((a, b) => a + b, 0) /
this.readings.length;
    })
  );

  readonly criticalAlert$: Observable<string | null> =
this.rawSensor$.pipe(
      map((temp) => (temp > 30 ? 'Temperature Critical!' : null))
  );

  constructor() {
    // Simulate sensor readings updating the signal
    setInterval(() => {
      const newTemp = 15 + Math.random() * 20;
      this.rawSensor.set(newTemp);
    }, 1000);
  }
}

// signals-to-observables.component.ts (Simplified - showcasing
usage)
import { Component, inject } from '@angular/core';
import { SensorService } from './sensor.service';
import { AsyncPipe, DecimalPipe } from '@angular/common';

@Component({
  selector: 'app-signals-to-observables-demo',
  imports: [AsyncPipe, DecimalPipe],
  template: `
    <!-- Display raw signal -->
    <p>Raw: {{ sensorService.rawSensor() }}°C</p>
    <!-- Display observables derived from signal -->
    <p>Stabilized: {{ sensorService.stabilizedTemp$ | async
```

```
}}°C</p>
    <p>Average: {{ sensorService.averageTemp$ | async }}°C</p>
    @if (sensorService.criticalAlert$ | async; as alert) {
      <p>Alert: {{ alert }}</p>
    }
  `,
  // ... other metadata
})
export class SignalsToObservablesComponent {
  protected readonly sensorService = inject(SensorService);
}
```

Explanation:

- **Import `toObservable`:** We import `toObservable` from `@angular/core/rxjs-interop`.
- **Signal Source:** We have the `rawSensor` Signal within the `SensorService`.
- **`toObservable()` Conversion:** We use `toObservable(this.rawSensor)` to create `rawSensor$`, an Observable that mirrors the `rawSensor` Signal's value.
- **RxJS Operators:** We can now chain standard RxJS operators (`debounceTime`, `distinctUntilChanged`, `map`) to the `rawSensor$` Observable to create derived Observables (`stabilizedTemp$`, `averageTemp$`, `criticalAlert$`).
- **Consumption:** A component (`SignalsToObservablesComponent`) can inject `SensorService` and subscribe to these Observables (e.g., using the `AsyncPipe` in the template) to display the processed sensor data.

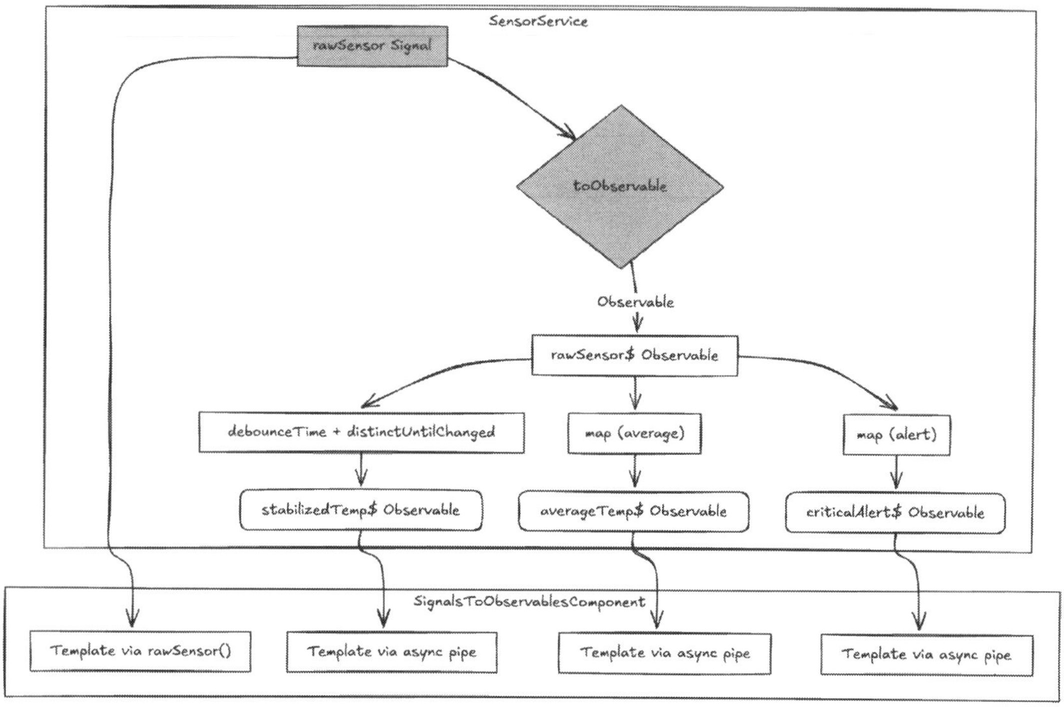

Figure 7.2 - Converting rawSensor signal to an observable using toObservable() method

`toObservable()` allows you to seamlessly integrate Signals into RxJS workflows, enabling you to leverage the vast ecosystem of RxJS operators and libraries while still benefiting from Signal-based state management at the source.

You can find the code of this example at `` `apps/chapter-07/src/app/signals-to-observables` ``. From the code repository root, run the following command to serve the project:

```
nx serve chapter-07
```

Then, navigate to ***http://localhost:4200/signals-to-obs*** to see the example

Best Practices for Using Observables with Signals

When working with both Observables and Signals in hybrid applications, consider these best practices:

- **Use `toSignal()` for Read-Only Consumption:** Employ `toSignal()` primarily when you need to consume data from Observables within your Signal-based components or computed values. This is ideal for displaying data from existing RxJS services or external sources reactively. Remember to provide an initialValue.
- **Use `toObservable()` for RxJS Integration:** Utilize `toObservable()` when you need to expose Signal values to RxJS-based logic, such as interacting with legacy services, using RxJS operators, or integrating with RxJS-heavy libraries.
- **Choose the Right Tool for the Job:** For new features and components, strongly consider using Signals for state management and reactivity. Reserve RxJS for complex asynchronous flows, event streams, or when interoperating with legacy code or libraries that heavily rely on it.
- **Minimize Conversions:** Avoid unnecessary back-and-forth conversions between Observables and Signals. Strategically choose the reactive model that best suits each part of your application to minimize overhead and maintain clarity.

Strategies for Migrating to Signals

Migrating a large, RxJS-based Angular application to Signals is a journey, not a sprint. A gradual, phased approach is crucial for minimizing disruption and ensuring application stability.

Gradual Adoption in a Large Codebase

Phase 1: Identify Migration Targets: Begin by identifying components and services that are relatively self-contained and would benefit most from Signal-based reactivity. Good candidates include:

- **Presentational Components:** Components primarily focused on displaying data and responding to user interactions, often with simpler state management logic.
- **Stateless Services:** Services that perform data transformations or calculations without managing complex internal state.
- **New Features:** When developing new features, adopt Signals from the outset wherever feasible.

Phase 2: Convert Local Component State: Start by refactoring the local state management within your chosen components to use Signals. Replace `BehaviorSubject` or state based state management with `signal()`. Convert component inputs and outputs to use the new `input()`, `output()`, and `model()` APIs.

Phase 3: Migrate Service Layers: Gradually migrate services to use Signals for internal state management. Refactor **BehaviorSubject**-based state in services to use `signal()` and `computed()`. Consider exposing service APIs as Signals where appropriate, using `toObservable()` if you need to maintain RxJS compatibility for existing consumers initially. Use `toSignal()` within services if they depend on other RxJS-based services.

Phase 4: Refactor Complex Observables: Address more complex RxJS logic incrementally. Identify areas where you can simplify intricate Observable chains by using computed Signals to derive values and effects to handle side effects. This phase might involve breaking down large Observables into smaller, more manageable Signals and effects.

Best Practices for Migrating Components and Services

- **Start Small and Iterate:** Begin with smaller, less critical components to gain experience and build confidence with Signals. Iterate and refine your migration approach as you progress.
- **Test Thoroughly:** Ensure comprehensive unit and integration tests are in place before and after each migration step. Signals often simplify testing, but rigorous testing remains paramount (as detailed in Chapter 8).
- **Focus on Performance Bottlenecks:** Prioritize migrating components and services that are known performance bottlenecks or areas with complex change detection logic. Signals' fine-grained reactivity can offer significant performance improvements in such areas.
- **Maintain Code Clarity:** As you mix Observables and Signals during migration, prioritize code clarity. Use comments and clear naming conventions (e.g., data$ for Observables, count for Signals) to distinguish between RxJS and Signal-based logic. Ensure your team understands both paradigms and the interoperability strategies (`toSignal`, `toObservable`).
- **Gradual Type Conversion:** When migrating from RxJS to Signals, you might encounter type mismatches. Use TypeScript's type casting or create intermediate Signals or Observables to bridge type differences during the transition.

Refactoring Complex Observables to Simpler Signals

One of the significant advantages of Signals is their ability to simplify complex reactive logic. During migration, look for opportunities to refactor intricate Observable chains into more declarative and easier-to-understand Signals and effects. For example, logic involving multiple `switchMap`, `combineLatest`, and `filter` operators might be significantly cleaner when expressed using a combination of `signal()`, `computed()`, and *potentially* `effect()`.

Working with Both Reactive Styles

During the migration process, your application will likely be a hybrid of RxJS and Signal-based code. It's essential to establish clear patterns and maintain code clarity when working with both reactive styles.

- **Establish Clear Boundaries:** Define clear boundaries between RxJS and Signal-based modules or components. This will help manage complexity and make it easier to reason about data flow.
- **Consistent Naming Conventions:** Adopt naming conventions to clearly distinguish between Observables (e.g., data$, userStream$) and Signals (e.g., count, userName). This improves code readability and reduces confusion.
- **Code Comments and Documentation:** Provide clear comments to explain the reactive logic, especially in hybrid sections of your codebase. Document the purpose of `toSignal()` and `toObservable()` conversions and the rationale behind using each reactive style in specific parts of the application.

Practical Example: Real-Time Dashboard Migration

Let's see a real-time dashboard example and illustrate a practical migration scenario. Imagine we have an existing dashboard component that uses Observables for fetching and displaying metrics. In this example, the `MetricsService` handles trend calculations internally and provides a combined stream.

Original Observable Implementation:

This version uses a shared stream (`metrics$`) from `MetricsService` which already includes trends. The component subscribes to this stream and uses `map` operators to extract the individual CPU/Memory values and trends for the template, consumed via `AsyncPipe`.

```
// metrics.service.ts (Simplified)
import { Injectable } from '@angular/core';
```

```
import { Observable, interval, switchMap, map, shareReplay, /* ...
*/ } from 'rxjs';

export interface Metrics {
  cpu: number;
  memory: number;
  trends: { cpu: number; memory: number; };
}

@Injectable({ providedIn: 'root' })
export class MetricsService {
  private previousValues = { cpu: 0, memory: 0 };

  // Single shared stream calculating and providing trends
  private metrics$ = interval(2000).pipe(
    switchMap(() => this.fetchMetrics()), // Fetch raw cpu/memory
    map(metrics => {
      // Calculate trends based on previous values
      const cpuTrend = metrics.cpu - this.previousValues.cpu;
      const memoryTrend = metrics.memory -
this.previousValues.memory;
      this.previousValues = { cpu: metrics.cpu, memory:
metrics.memory }; // Update history
      // Return metrics object including trends
      return { ...metrics, trends: { cpu: cpuTrend, memory:
memoryTrend } };
    }),
    shareReplay(1) // Share the result
  );

  getMetrics(): Observable<Metrics> {
    return this.metrics$; // Components consume the shared stream
  }

  private fetchMetrics(): Observable<{ cpu: number; memory: number
}> {
     // Simulate fetching raw data
     return of({ cpu: Math.random() * 100, memory: Math.random() *
100 }).pipe(delay(500));
  }
}
```

```
// dashboard.component.ts (Original - RxJS)
import { Component, inject, OnDestroy } from '@angular/core';
import { map, Subject, takeUntil } from 'rxjs';
import { MetricsService } from './metrics.service';
import { AsyncPipe } from '@angular/common';
import { MetricCardComponent } from './metric-card.component';

@Component({
  selector: 'app-dashboard',
  imports: [AsyncPipe, MetricCardComponent],
  template: `
    <div class="bg-base-300 p-4">
      <h2 class="text-3xl text-center mb-4">RxJS
Implementation</h2>
      <div class="grid grid-cols-2 gap-4">
        <app-metric-card title="CPU Usage"
          [value]="(cpuUsage$ | async) ?? 0"
          [trend]="(cpuTrend$ | async) ?? 0" />
        <app-metric-card title="Memory Usage"
          [value]="(memoryUsage$ | async) ?? 0"
          [trend]="(memoryTrend$ | async) ?? 0" />
      </div>
    </div>
  `,
})
export class DashboardComponent implements OnDestroy {
  private metricsService = inject(MetricsService);
  private destroy$ = new Subject<void>();

  // Consume the single shared stream from the service
  metrics$ =
this.metricsService.getMetrics().pipe(takeUntil(this.destroy$));

  // Use 'map' to extract specific values for the template
  cpuUsage$ = this.metrics$.pipe(map(m => m.cpu));
  memoryUsage$ = this.metrics$.pipe(map(m => m.memory));
  cpuTrend$ = this.metrics$.pipe(map(m => m.trends.cpu));
  memoryTrend$ = this.metrics$.pipe(map(m => m.trends.memory));

  ngOnDestroy(): void {
```

```
    this.destroy$.next();
    this.destroy$.complete();
  }
}
```

Migrated Signal Implementation:

This version migrates the state management to Signals. It subscribes to the same shared **`metrics$`** stream from the service. When new Metrics data arrives, it updates a single metrics Signal. Computed signals (**`cpuUsage`**, **`memoryUsage`**, **`cpuTrend`**, **`memoryTrend`**) are then used to derive the specific values needed by the template directly from this **`metrics`** Signal.

```
// dashboard-signal.component.ts (Migrated - Signals)
import { Component, inject, computed, signal } from
'@angular/core';
import { MetricsService, Metrics } from './metrics.service';
import { MetricCardComponent } from './metric-card.component';
import { takeUntilDestroyed } from '@angular/core/rxjs-interop';

@Component({
  selector: 'app-dashboard-signal',
  imports: [MetricCardComponent],
  template: `
    <div class="bg-base-300 p-4">
      <h2 class="text-3xl text-center mb-4">Signals
Implementation</h2>
      <div class="grid grid-cols-2 gap-4">
        <app-metric-card title="CPU Usage"
          [value]="cpuUsage()"
          [trend]="cpuTrend()" />
        <app-metric-card title="Memory Usage"
          [value]="memoryUsage()"
          [trend]="memoryTrend()" />
      </div>
    </div>
  `,
})
export class DashboardSignalComponent {
  private metricsService = inject(MetricsService);
```

```
  // Single signal holding the complete Metrics state
  metrics = signal<Metrics>({ cpu: 0, memory: 0, trends: { cpu: 0,
memory: 0 } });

  // Computed signals derive values directly from the 'metrics'
signal
  cpuUsage = computed(() => this.metrics().cpu);
  memoryUsage = computed(() => this.metrics().memory);
  cpuTrend = computed(() => this.metrics().trends.cpu);
  memoryTrend = computed(() => this.metrics().trends.memory);

  constructor() {
    // Subscribe to the shared stream from the service
    this.metricsService.getMetrics()
      .pipe(takeUntilDestroyed()) // Auto-unsubscribe on destroy
      .subscribe(latestMetrics => {
        // Update the single signal with the full metrics object
        this.metrics.set(latestMetrics);
      });
  }
}
```

You can find the code of this example at `` `apps/chapter-07/src/app/dashboard-migration` ``. From the code repository root, run the following command to serve the project:

```
nx serve chapter-07
```

Then, navigate to ***http://localhost:4200/dashboard-migration*** to see the example

Key Changes Reflected in the Update:

- **Centralized Logic:** The `MetricsService` now handles trend calculation, providing a cleaner, combined Metrics object via a single shared Observable (`metrics$`).
- **Simplified RxJS Component:** The `DashboardComponent` still uses RxJS but is simpler, primarily using map to extract data from the service's stream.

- **Signal Component:** The `DashboardSignalComponent` subscribes to the service's Observable once. It updates a single `metrics` Signal with the complete data.
- **Computed Derivations:** All values needed by the template (`cpuUsage`, `memoryUsage`, `cpuTrend`, `memoryTrend`) are now computed signals derived efficiently from the main metrics signal. This eliminates the need for separate trend signals and update logic within the component's subscription.
- **Template Consumption:** The RxJS template uses `async` pipe, while the Signal template uses direct accessor functions (`cpuUsage()`, `cpuTrend()`, etc.).

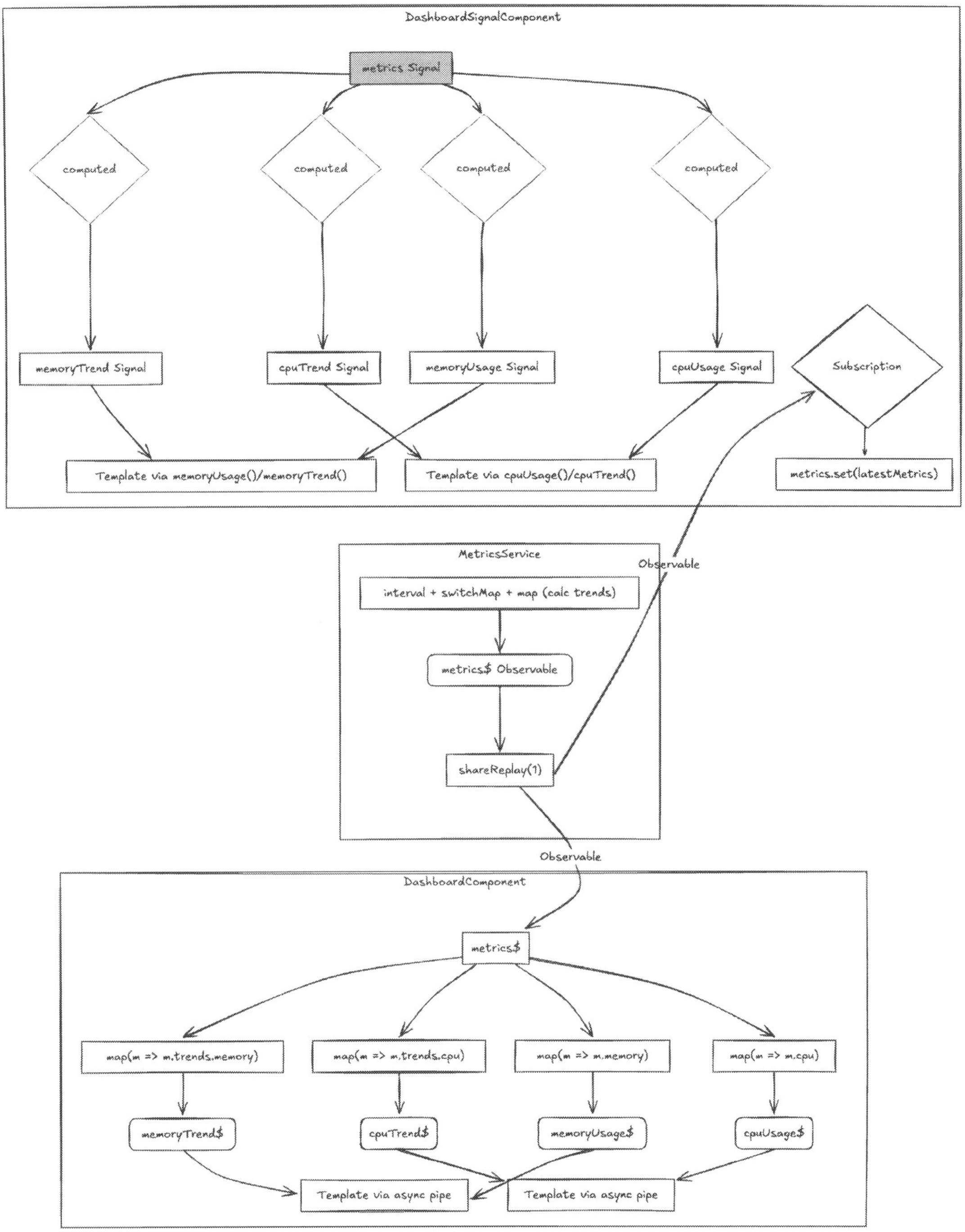

Figure 7.3 - Signals vs Observables approach to display metrics in a Dashboard

This example demonstrates a hybrid approach where we retain RxJS for interval-based polling (a common use case for Observables) but leverage Signals for managing and deriving component state, resulting in a more efficient and maintainable component.

Conclusion

This chapter has equipped you with the knowledge and strategies to navigate the interoperability landscape of Angular Signals and RxJS Observables. By understanding `toSignal()` and `toObservable()`, adopting a gradual migration approach, and focusing on code clarity, you can effectively integrate Signals into existing RxJS-based applications. Remember, migration is a journey of incremental improvements. Embrace the hybrid approach, strategically adopt Signals where they bring the most benefit, and gradually refactor your codebase towards a more signal-centric architecture.

In the next chapter, we will focus on a critical aspect of adopting Signals: **testing**. We will explore effective testing strategies for signal-based components and services, ensuring the reliability and robustness of your applications during and after migration.

Chapter 8: Testing with Signals

Introduction

As we embrace how cool Signals are for Angular applications, robust testing becomes even more critical. The fine-grained reactivity of Signals demands meticulous testing strategies to ensure our components and services behave as expected under various conditions. This chapter will equip you with the techniques and best practices to confidently test your Signal-based Angular code, ensuring application stability and maintainability.

Unit Testing Strategies

Basic Signal Testing

The fundamental principle of unit testing remains the same: isolate the unit under test (a component or service) and verify its behavior. When dealing with Signals, this often involves checking how Signals are initialized, updated, and how they influence other parts of the component or service.

Let's start with a basic example. We'll revisit our `CounterComponent`.

```
// counter.component.ts (Simplified)
import { Component, signal } from '@angular/core';

@Component({
  selector: 'app-counter',
  template: `
    <button (click)="decrement()">-</button>
    <div data-testid="countValue">{{ count() }}</div>
    <button (click)="increment()">+</button>
  `,
})
export class CounterComponent {
  count = signal(0);

  increment() { this.count.update(v => v + 1); }
  decrement() { this.count.update(v => Math.max(0, v - 1)); }
}
```

Here's how we can unit test it:

```
// counter.component.spec.ts (Simplified)
import { ComponentFixture, TestBed } from '@angular/core/testing';
import { CounterComponent } from './counter.component';

describe('CounterComponent', () => {
  let component: CounterComponent;
  let fixture: ComponentFixture<CounterComponent>;

  beforeEach(async () => {
    await TestBed.configureTestingModule({
      imports: [CounterComponent], // Import standalone component
    }).compileComponents();

    fixture = TestBed.createComponent(CounterComponent);
    component = fixture.componentInstance;
    fixture.detectChanges(); // Initial binding and render
  });

  it('should initialize count to 0', () => {
    expect(component.count()).toBe(0);
  });

  it('should increment count on increment()', () => {
    component.increment();
    expect(component.count()).toBe(1);
  });

  it('should decrement count on decrement() but not below 0', () =>
{
    component.increment(); // count is 1
    component.decrement(); // count is 0
    expect(component.count()).toBe(0);
    component.decrement(); // Try to decrement below 0
    expect(component.count()).toBe(0); // Stays 0
  });

  it('should update the view when count changes', () => {
    component.increment();
    fixture.detectChanges(); // Trigger change detection to update
```

```
the view

    const countValEl =
fixture.nativeElement.querySelector('[data-testid="countValue"]');
    expect(countValEl.textContent.trim()).toBe('1');
  });
});
```

You can find the code of this example at `apps/chapter-08/src/app/counter`. From the code repository root, run the following command to serve the project:

```
nx serve chapter-08
```

Then, navigate to ***http://localhost:4200/counter*** to see the example

To run the tests, run the following command:

```
nx test chapter-08 -t "Counter"
```

Explanation:

- **Basic Setup:** We use TestBed to configure the testing module and create a component fixture.
- **Initial State:** We verify that the count Signal is correctly initialized to 0 by calling `component.count()`.
- **Action Verification:** We call the `increment()` and `decrement()` methods and assert that the count Signal is updated accordingly by accessing its value again.
- `detectChanges()`: Calling `fixture.detectChanges()` after the component is created binds the signal to the template and renders its initial value. Crucially, even though Signals are reactive, we still need to call `fixture.detectChanges()` after we perform an action (like `component.increment()`) if we want to test the result in the template. This tells Angular to run its change detection cycle and update the DOM based on the latest signal values.
- **data-testid:** We use the `data-testid` attribute to reliably select the specific HTML element displaying the counter's value. This is a best practice for testing, as it decouples tests from CSS classes or structural

changes.

Testing Computed Signals

Computed signals derive their values from other signals. Testing them involves ensuring they are initialized correctly and update automatically when their dependencies change. Let's use the **`FullNameComponent`**.

```
// full-name.component.ts (Simplified)
import { Component, signal, computed } from '@angular/core';
import { FormsModule } from '@angular/forms'; // Needed for ngModel

@Component({
  selector: 'app-full-name',
  imports: [FormsModule], // Import FormsModule
  template: `
    <input data-testid="firstName"
[(ngModel)]="formValues.firstName" />
    <input data-testid="lastName" [(ngModel)]="formValues.lastName"
/>
    <p data-testid="fullName">Full name: {{ fullName() }}</p>
  `,
})
export class FullNameComponent {
  formValues = {
    firstName: signal('John'),
    lastName: signal('Doe'),
  };
  fullName = computed(
    () => `${this.formValues.firstName()}
${this.formValues.lastName()}`
  );
}
```

Testing this component:

```
// full-name.component.spec.ts (Simplified)
import { ComponentFixture, TestBed } from '@angular/core/testing';
import { FullNameComponent } from './full-name.component';
// No need to import FormsModule here if it's imported by the
```

```
component

describe('FullNameComponent', () => {
  let component: FullNameComponent;
  let fixture: ComponentFixture<FullNameComponent>;

  beforeEach(async () => {
    await TestBed.configureTestingModule({
      imports: [FullNameComponent], // Import standalone component
    }).compileComponents();

    fixture = TestBed.createComponent(FullNameComponent);
    component = fixture.componentInstance;
    fixture.detectChanges();
  });

  it('should initialize fullName correctly', () => {
    expect(component.fullName()).toBe('John Doe');
  });

  it('should update fullName when firstName changes', () => {
    component.formValues.firstName.set('Jane');
    // No detectChanges needed here as we test the computed signal
directly
    expect(component.fullName()).toBe('Jane Doe');
  });

  it('should update fullName when lastName changes', () => {
    component.formValues.lastName.set('Smith');
    expect(component.fullName()).toBe('John Smith');
  });

  it('should reflect changes in the view', () => {
    component.formValues.firstName.set('Jane');
    component.formValues.lastName.set('Smith');
    fixture.detectChanges(); // Needed to update the template

    const element =
fixture.nativeElement.querySelector('[data-testid="fullName"]');
    expect(element.textContent.trim()).toBe('Full name: Jane
Smith');
```

```
  });
});
```

You can find the code of this example at `apps/chapter-08/src/app/full-name`. From the code repository root, run the following command to serve the project:

nx serve chapter-08

Then, navigate to ***http://localhost:4200/full-name*** to see the example

To run the tests, run the following command:

nx test chapter-08 -t "FullName"

Explanation:

- **Initial Value:** We check the initial computed value of fullName().
- **Dependency Updates:** We directly `.set()` new values on the dependency signals (firstName, lastName) and assert that the `fullName()` computed signal automatically reflects the change without needing `detectChanges()` for the assertion on the signal itself.
- **View Update:** We verify that after changing the dependency signals and calling `detectChanges()`, the template correctly displays the updated computed value.

Testing Effects

Effects perform side effects when their dependent signals change. Testing them requires verifying that these side effects occur as expected. This often involves mocking dependencies or spying on external interactions (like console.log, DOM manipulation, or service calls).

Let's enhance our `SignupFormComponent` (simplified) to include an effect that logs validity.

```
// signup-form.component.ts (Simplified with effect)
import { Component, model, computed, effect } from '@angular/core';
import { FormsModule } from '@angular/forms';
import { NgIf } from '@angular/common';
```

```
@Component({
  selector: 'app-signup-form',
  standalone: true,
  imports: [FormsModule, NgIf],
  template: `
    <form (ngSubmit)="onSubmit()">
      <input type="email" [(ngModel)]="email" name="email" required
/>
      <input type="password" [(ngModel)]="password" name="password"
required />
      <button type="submit" [disabled]="!isFormValid()">Sign
Up</button>
    </form>
  `,
})
export class SignupFormComponent {
  email = model('');
  password = model('');
  // ... computed signals for errors and validity ...
  isFormValid = computed(() => /* ... validation logic ... */
true);

  constructor() {
    effect(() => {
      // Effect depends on isFormValid computed signal
      console.log('Form validity changed:', this.isFormValid());
    });
  }
  onSubmit() { /* ... */}
}
```

Testing the effect:

```
// signup-form.component.spec.ts (Simplified - testing effect)
import { ComponentFixture, TestBed } from '@angular/core/testing';
import { FormsModule } from '@angular/forms';
import { SignupFormComponent } from './signup-form.component';

describe('SignupFormComponent Effect', () => {
  let component: SignupFormComponent;
  let fixture: ComponentFixture<SignupFormComponent>;
```

```
  let consoleSpy: jest.SpyInstance; // Use jest.SpyInstance for
Jest

  beforeEach(async () => {
    await TestBed.configureTestingModule({
      imports: [SignupFormComponent, FormsModule],
    }).compileComponents();

    // Spy on console.log BEFORE component creation/detection
    // so the initial effect run is captured if needed.
    consoleSpy = jest.spyOn(console, 'log').mockImplementation(()
=> {}); // Mock impl to prevent actual logging

    fixture = TestBed.createComponent(SignupFormComponent);
    component = fixture.componentInstance;
    fixture.detectChanges(); // This triggers the initial run of
the effect
  });

  afterEach(() => {
    consoleSpy.mockRestore(); // Clean up the spy
  });

  it('should log form validity changes', () => {
    // Effect runs once on init (called by detectChanges in
beforeEach)
    expect(consoleSpy).toHaveBeenCalledWith('Form validity
changed:', false); // Assuming initial state is invalid

    consoleSpy.mockClear(); // Clear previous calls before
triggering change

    // Make the form valid
    component.email.set('test@example.com');
    component.password.set('validpassword123');
    fixture.detectChanges(); // Allow computed signals and effect
to run

    // Assert the effect logged the new state
    expect(consoleSpy).toHaveBeenCalledWith('Form validity
changed:', true);
```

```
  });
});
```

You can find the code of this example at `apps/chapter-08/src/app/signup-form`. From the code repository root, run the following command to serve the project:

nx serve chapter-08

Then, navigate to ***http://localhost:4200/signup-form*** to see the example

To run the tests, run the following command:

nx test chapter-08 -t "SignupForm"

Explanation:

- **Spying:** We use `jest.spyOn(console, 'log')` (or the equivalent for your test runner, like Jasmine's spyOn) to intercept calls to console.log. We spy before `fixture.detectChanges()` to capture the effect's initial run.
- **Triggering Change:** We modify the signals (`email`, `password`) that the `isFormValid` computed signal depends on.
- `detectChanges()`: We call `detectChanges()` to ensure Angular processes the signal changes, re-evaluates the computed signal, and triggers the effect.
- **Assertion:** We assert that our `consoleSpy` was called with the expected arguments, verifying the effect ran correctly.
- **Cleanup:** Using `mockRestore()` (Jest) or `spy.and.callThrough()` (Jasmine, if needed) in `afterEach` is good practice.

Testing Asynchronous Operations (rxResource)

Testing components or services using resource or `rxResource` involves handling asynchronous data loading, success states, and error states. Mocking the service providing the data is essential. Let's test the WeatherInfoComponent which uses rxResource.

```
// weather.service.ts (Simplified)
import { Injectable } from '@angular/core';
```

```
import { HttpClient } from '@angular/common/http';
import { Observable, delay } from 'rxjs';

interface WeatherData { /* ... */ }

@Injectable({ providedIn: 'root' })
export class WeatherService {
  constructor(private http: HttpClient) {}
  getWeather(): Observable<WeatherData> {
    return
this.http.get<WeatherData>('assets/weather.json').pipe(delay(500));
// Simulates delay
  }
}

// weather-info.component.ts (Simplified)
import { Component, inject } from '@angular/core';
import { rxResource } from '@angular/core/rxjs-interop';
import { WeatherService } from './weather.service';
import { catchError } from 'rxjs';

interface WeatherData { /* ... */ }

@Component({
  selector: 'app-weather-info',
  template: `
    <button (click)="weatherResource.reload()">Reload</button>
    @if (weatherResource.isLoading()) { <span
data-testid="weatherLoader">Loading...</span> }
    @else if (weatherResource.error()) { <div
data-testid="weatherError">Error: {{ weatherResource.error()
}}</div> }
    @else if (weatherResource.value(); as weather) {
      <div data-testid="weatherData">
        Temp: {{ weather.temperature }}, Cond: {{ weather.condition
}}
      </div>
    }
  `,
})
export class WeatherInfoComponent {
```

```
  weatherService = inject(WeatherService);
  weatherResource = rxResource<WeatherData, string>({
    stream: () => this.weatherService.getWeather().pipe(
        catchError(() => { throw 'Could not fetch data'; }) //
Simplified error throwing
      ),
  });
}
```

Testing with **`fakeAsync`** and **`tick`**:

```
// weather-info.component.spec.ts (Simplified)
import { ComponentFixture, TestBed, fakeAsync, tick } from
'@angular/core/testing';
import { WeatherInfoComponent } from './weather-info.component';
import { WeatherService, WeatherData } from './weather.service';
import { of, throwError } from 'rxjs';

describe('WeatherInfoComponent (rxResource)', () => {
  let component: WeatherInfoComponent;
  let fixture: ComponentFixture<WeatherInfoComponent>;
  // Use jest.Mocked for stricter typing with Jest spies
  let weatherServiceMock: jest.Mocked<WeatherService>;

  beforeEach(() => {
    // Create a mock object with the required methods
    weatherServiceMock = {
        getWeather: jest.fn()
    } as jest.Mocked<WeatherService>;

    TestBed.configureTestingModule({
      imports: [WeatherInfoComponent],
      providers: [
        // Provide the mock service instead of the real one
        { provide: WeatherService, useValue: weatherServiceMock },
      ],
    });

    fixture = TestBed.createComponent(WeatherInfoComponent);
    component = fixture.componentInstance;
```

```
    // DON'T call detectChanges yet if the resource loads
immediately
  });

  it('should display loading state initially', () => {
      // Setup the mock BEFORE detectChanges triggers the resource
load
      weatherServiceMock.getWeather.mockReturnValue(of({
temperature: 25, condition: 'Sunny', icon: '' }).pipe(delay(500)));
// Simulate delay

      fixture.detectChanges(); // Now trigger resource load

      expect(component.weatherResource.isLoading()).toBe(true);

expect(fixture.nativeElement.querySelector('[data-testid="weatherLo
ader"]')).toBeTruthy();
  });

  it('should display weather data after loading', fakeAsync(() => {
    const mockWeatherData = { temperature: 25, condition: 'Sunny',
icon: '' };
    // Setup the mock to return data after a delay

weatherServiceMock.getWeather.mockReturnValue(of(mockWeatherData).p
ipe(delay(100))); // Use a delay

    fixture.detectChanges(); // Trigger resource load

    expect(component.weatherResource.isLoading()).toBe(true);

    tick(100); // Advance time to cover the delay in the mock
service
    fixture.detectChanges(); // Update view with loaded data

    expect(component.weatherResource.isLoading()).toBe(false);

expect(component.weatherResource.value()).toEqual(mockWeatherData);
    const dataDiv =
fixture.nativeElement.querySelector('[data-testid="weatherData"]');
    expect(dataDiv.textContent).toContain('Temp: 25, Cond: Sunny');
```

```
  }));

  it('should display error message on error', fakeAsync(() => {
      const errorMsg = 'Could not fetch data';
      // Setup the mock to return an error after a delay
      weatherServiceMock.getWeather.mockReturnValue(throwError(()
=> errorMsg).pipe(delay(100)));

      fixture.detectChanges(); // Trigger resource load
      expect(component.weatherResource.isLoading()).toBe(true);

      tick(100); // Advance time
      fixture.detectChanges(); // Update view with error state

      expect(component.weatherResource.isLoading()).toBe(false);
      expect(component.weatherResource.error()).toBe(errorMsg);
      const errorDiv =
fixture.nativeElement.querySelector('[data-testid="weatherError"]')
;
      expect(errorDiv.textContent).toContain(`Error: ${errorMsg}`);
  }));
});
```

You can find the code of this example at **`` `apps/chapter-08/src/app/weather` ``**. From the code repository root, run the following command to serve the project:

`nx serve chapter-08`

Then, navigate to ***http://localhost:4200/weather*** to see the example

To run the tests, run the following command:

`nx test chapter-08 -t "Weather"`

Explanation:

- **Mocking Service:** We create a mock **`WeatherService`** using **`jest.fn()`** (or Jasmine's **`createSpyObj`**) and provide it using TestBed. This lets us control what the getWeather method returns in each test.

- **`fakeAsync` and `tick`:** We wrap asynchronous tests in `fakeAsync`. This allows us to control the passage of time using `tick`(milliseconds). We use `tick()` to simulate the delay introduced by the service (or the delay operator in our mock).
- **Controlling Mock Return:** Inside each test, we configure the `weatherServiceMock.getWeather` spy to return either a successful Observable (`of(...)`) or an erroring Observable (`throwError(...)`), often combined with a `delay()` to mimic network latency.
- **Testing States:** We assert the different states of the `weatherResource` (`isLoading(), error(), value()`) directly on the component instance and also check the template for the corresponding loading/error/data messages.
- **`detectChanges()` Timing:** We call `detectChanges()` initially to trigger the resource load (if it loads on init) and again after calling `tick()` to update the template with the resolved data or error state.

Testing Components with New Signal APIs

Let's examine testing components using `input()`, `output()`, and `model()`.

Testing input()

Consider ProfileComponent using the `input()` API.

```
// profile.component.ts (Simplified)
import { Component, input } from '@angular/core';
interface User { name: string; age: number; }

@Component({
  selector: 'app-profile',
  template: `@if(user()) { <div><p>Name: {{ user()?.name
}}</p><p>Age: {{ user()?.age }}</p></div> }`,
})
export class ProfileComponent {
  user = input<User>(); // Required input would be
input.required<User>()
}

@Component({
  selector: 'app-profile-example',
  template: ` <app-profile [user]="user"></app-profile> `,
  imports: [ProfileComponent],
```

```
})
export class ProfileExampleComponent {
  user: User = {
    name: 'John Doe',
    age: 30,
  };
}
```

Testing this involves setting the input value on the component instance or fixture.

```
// profile.component.spec.ts (Simplified)
import { ComponentFixture, TestBed } from '@angular/core/testing';
import { ProfileComponent } from './profile.component';

describe('ProfileComponent Input', () => {
  let fixture: ComponentFixture<ProfileComponent>;

  beforeEach(() => {
    TestBed.configureTestingModule({ imports: [ProfileComponent]
});
    fixture = TestBed.createComponent(ProfileComponent);
    // Don't detectChanges here if you want to test the initial
undefined state
  });

  it('should display user data when input is provided', () => {
    const testUser = { name: 'Alice', age: 30 };

    // Set input value using fixture.componentRef.setInput
    fixture.componentRef.setInput('user', testUser);
    fixture.detectChanges(); // Update the template

    const element: HTMLElement = fixture.nativeElement;
    expect(element.textContent).toContain('Name: Alice');
    expect(element.textContent).toContain('Age: 30');
  });

   it('should update view when input changes', () => {
     fixture.componentRef.setInput('user', { name: 'Alice', age: 30
```

```
});
    fixture.detectChanges();

    fixture.componentRef.setInput('user', { name: 'Bob', age: 25
});
    fixture.detectChanges(); // Re-run change detection

    const element: HTMLElement = fixture.nativeElement;
    expect(element.textContent).toContain('Name: Bob');
    expect(element.textContent).toContain('Age: 25');
  });
});
```

You can find the code of this example at `` `apps/chapter-08/src/app/profile` ``. From the code repository root, run the following command to serve the project:

`nx serve chapter-08`

Then, navigate to ***http://localhost:4200/profile*** to see the example

To run the tests, run the following command:

`nx test chapter-08 -t "Profile"`

Explanation:

- **Setting Input:** The preferred way to set Signal inputs in tests is `fixture.componentRef.setInput('inputPropertyName', value)`. This correctly triggers Angular's mechanisms.
- `detectChanges()`: Call `detectChanges()` after setting the input to update the component's view.
- **Assertion:** Verify the template renders the correct data based on the provided input.

Testing output()

Consider `MyButtonComponent` using the `output()` API.

```
// my-button.component.ts (Simplified)
```

```
import { Component, output } from '@angular/core';

@Component({
  selector: 'app-my-button',
  template: `<button data-testid="myButton"
(click)="onClick()">Click Me</button>`,
})
export class MyButtonComponent {
  clicked = output<void>(); // No generic type needed for void
emission

  onClick() {
    this.clicked.emit();
  }
}
```

Testing involves spying on the output's emit method.

```
// my-button.component.spec.ts (Simplified)
import { ComponentFixture, TestBed } from '@angular/core/testing';
import { MyButtonComponent } from './my-button.component';

describe('MyButtonComponent Output', () => {
  let component: MyButtonComponent;
  let fixture: ComponentFixture<MyButtonComponent>;

  beforeEach(() => {
    TestBed.configureTestingModule({ imports: [MyButtonComponent]
});
    fixture = TestBed.createComponent(MyButtonComponent);
    component = fixture.componentInstance;
    fixture.detectChanges();
  });

  it('should emit clicked event when button is clicked', () => {
    // Spy directly on the output property
    const clickedSpy = jest.spyOn(component.clicked, 'emit');

    const button =
fixture.nativeElement.querySelector('[data-testid="myButton"]');
```

```
    button.click(); // Simulate the click

    expect(clickedSpy).toHaveBeenCalledTimes(1);
    // For outputs with values:
expect(clickedSpy).toHaveBeenCalledWith(expectedValue);
  });
});
```

You can find the code of this example at `apps/chapter-08/src/app/my-button`. From the code repository root, run the following command to serve the project:

```
nx serve chapter-08
```

Then, navigate to ***http://localhost:4200/my-button*** to see the example

To run the tests, run the following command:

```
nx test chapter-08 -t "MyButton"
```

Explanation:

- **Spy on emit:** We use `jest.spyOn(component.clicked, 'emit')` to spy on the `emit` method of the `output` signal instance.
- **Simulate Action:** We find the button in the template and simulate a click event.
- **Assert Emission:** We verify that the spy (`clickedSpy`) was called.

Testing model()

Consider MyInputComponent using the model() API for two-way binding.

```
// my-input.component.ts (Simplified)
import { Component, model } from '@angular/core';
import { FormsModule } from '@angular/forms'; // Needed for ngModel

@Component({
  selector: 'app-my-input',
  standalone: true,
  imports: [FormsModule],
```

```
  template: `
      <input type="text" [(ngModel)]="text" data-testid="myInput"/>
      <p data-testid="myPreview">Current value: {{ text() }}</p>
  `,
})
export class MyInputComponent {
  text = model<string>(''); // Two-way bound signal
}
```

Testing **`model()`** often involves checking both directions: does the component update when the input element changes, and does the input element update when the model is set programmatically?

```
// my-input.component.spec.ts (Simplified)
import { ComponentFixture, TestBed } from '@angular/core/testing';
import { FormsModule } from '@angular/forms';
import { MyInputComponent } from './my-input.component';

describe('MyInputComponent Model', () => {
  let component: MyInputComponent;
  let fixture: ComponentFixture<MyInputComponent>;

  beforeEach(() => {
    TestBed.configureTestingModule({
      imports: [MyInputComponent, FormsModule],
    });
    fixture = TestBed.createComponent(MyInputComponent);
    component = fixture.componentInstance;
    fixture.detectChanges();
  });

  it('should update text model when input element changes', () => {
    const inputEl =
fixture.nativeElement.querySelector('[data-testid="myInput"]') as
HTMLInputElement;
    const previewEl =
fixture.nativeElement.querySelector('[data-testid="myPreview"]');

    inputEl.value = 'New Text';
    inputEl.dispatchEvent(new Event('input')); // Simulate user
```

```
input
    fixture.detectChanges();

    expect(component.text()).toBe('New Text');
    expect(previewEl.textContent).toContain('New Text');
  });

  // Test the other direction (programmatic change reflected in
input value)
  // Note: Testing [(ngModel)] reflection requires fakeAsync/tick
or async/await fixture.whenStable
  it('should update input element value when model is set
programmatically', fakeAsync(() => {
      const inputEl =
fixture.nativeElement.querySelector('[data-testid="myInput"]') as
HTMLInputElement;

      component.text.set('Programmatic Update');
      fixture.detectChanges(); // Detect changes to update binding
      tick(); // Allow time for ngModel internal updates
      fixture.detectChanges(); // Detect changes again to reflect
in input value

      expect(inputEl.value).toBe('Programmatic Update');
  }));
});
```

You can find the code of this example at `` `apps/chapter-08/src/app/my-input` ``. From the code repository root, run the following command to serve the project:

```
nx serve chapter-08
```

Then, navigate to ***http://localhost:4200/my-input*** to see the example

To run the tests, run the following command:

```
nx test chapter-08 -t "MyInput"
```

Explanation:

- **Input -> Model:** We simulate changing the input element's value and dispatching an input event. We then verify that the `component.text()` signal has been updated.
- **Model -> Input:** We programmatically set the model using `component.text.set()`. Because `[(ngModel)]` involves asynchronous updates, we often need `fakeAsync/tick` or `async/await fixture.whenStable()` to ensure the input element's value property reflects the change before asserting. We call `detectChanges()` twice around the tick to ensure Angular processes the model change and then updates the view binding.

Practical Example: Testing the Signup Form

The SignupFormComponent tests combine many of these techniques:

- Testing `model()` signals (`email`, `password`).
- Testing `computed()` signals (`emailErrors`, `passwordErrors`, `isFormValid`, `submitButtonText`).
- Testing **DOM** elements (checking error messages, button **disabled** state).
- Testing effects (spying on console.log).
- Testing asynchronous operations within onSubmit (using `fakeAsync/tick`).
- Review the `signup-form.component.spec.ts` file provided earlier for the comprehensive tests covering these scenarios. Key aspects include:
- Setting model values (`component.email.set(...)`).
- Checking computed signal values (`expect(component.emailErrors()).toBe(...)`).
- Querying DOM elements based on `data-testid` to check for errors or button states.
- Simulating form submission (`form.dispatchEvent(new Event('ngSubmit'))`).
- Using `fakeAsync/tick` to test the simulated API call within onSubmit.
- Spying on `console.log` to verify effect execution.

Conclusion

This chapter provided a comprehensive guide to testing Angular components and services that utilize Signals. We covered testing basic signals, computed signals, effects, asynchronous operations with `rxResource`, and the new `input`, `output`, and `model` APIs. Key takeaways include leveraging `TestBed`, mocking dependencies, using spies, understanding when `detectChanges()` is necessary, and employing `fakeAsync/tick` for asynchronous scenarios. By applying these strategies, you can ensure the reliability and maintainability of your Signal-based Angular applications. Remember that thorough testing is crucial when working with the inherent reactivity of Signals.

In the next chapter, we'll explore performance considerations when using Signals and dive into some advanced use cases and architectural patterns.

Chapter 9: Performance and Advanced Use-Cases

Introduction

In the previous chapters, we've established a solid foundation for using Angular Signals to manage state and reactivity. Signals can significantly simplify your data flow and state management, leading to cleaner and more understandable code. They also bring inherent performance benefits due to Angular's refined mechanisms for detecting changes more granularly[. As Angular applications grow in complexity, understanding how to optimize performance further and leverage advanced Signal concepts becomes essential for building truly efficient and scalable solutions.

This chapter will dive deeper into the performance aspects of Signals in Angular. We'll explore advanced patterns for structuring your application and reusing logic effectively. We will look at how to fine-tune your application for optimal performance, discuss common pitfalls, and cover strategies for troubleshooting.

By the end of this chapter, you will be able to:

- Understand the performance benefits (and potential pitfalls) of using Signals[.
- Leverage advanced Signal patterns for reusable logic.
- Incorporate architectural patterns to structure your Signal-based applications effectively.
- Troubleshoot common issues and handle errors gracefully in computed and effect blocks.

Let's get started!

Performance Considerations

1. Fine-Tuning Performance with Signals

Angular's change detection mechanism determines how and when the UI updates in response to state changes. Signals integrate neatly into this, enabling more precise updates: only components reading a changed signal are typically marked for checking. By default, Signals are optimized to notify consumers only when their value actually changes (using === comparison).

While Signals offer significant improvements, especially paving the way for potential *"zoneless"* applications with even finer-grained updates[, additional attention to design can yield greater benefits.

1.1 Minimizing Computed Signal Chains

Computed signals can depend on other computed signals, creating chains (**Signal A -> Computed B -> Computed C**). While useful for encapsulation, deep chains can sometimes complicate debugging. Although Angular's caching prevents re-computation unless dependencies change, overly complex chains might slightly obscure data flow.

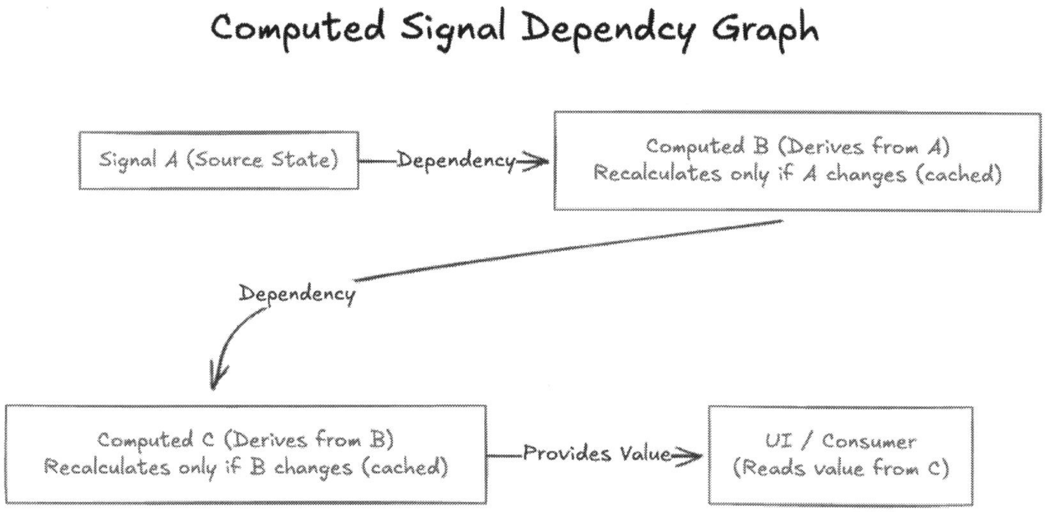

Figure 9.1 - Example of computed signals' dependency graph

Best Practice: Prefer flatter dependency graphs where possible. Break down complex, multi-step derivations into smaller, more focused computed signals. This enhances testability and maintainability.

1.2 Using Derived Signals Effectively

Computed signals are memoized (cached). If you repeatedly filter or transform data from a source signal in multiple places, create a single computed signal for that derivation. This leverages caching and avoids redundant calculations.

Consider filtering active users from a user list signal:

```
// user.service.ts (Simplified Example)
import { Injectable, signal, computed } from '@angular/core';
```

```
interface User { id: number; name: string; isActive: boolean; }

@Injectable({ providedIn: 'root' })
export class UserService {
  private usersList = signal<User[]>([ /* ...initial users... */
]);

  // Computed signal for active users - calculated only when
usersList changes
  activeUsers = computed(() => {
    console.log('Recalculating active users...'); // Logs only when
usersList changes
    return this.usersList().filter(u => u.isActive);
  });

  // Method to update the source signal
  toggleUserStatus(userId: number) {
    this.usersList.update(users =>
      users.map(u => u.id === userId ? { ...u, isActive:
!u.isActive } : u)
    );
  }
}

// Component consuming the computed signal
import { Component, inject } from '@angular/core';
import { UserService } from './user.service';

@Component({ /* ... */ })
export class ActiveUserListComponent {
  userService = inject(UserService);
  // Directly use the computed signal. The filtering logic is in
the service.
  activeUsers = this.userService.activeUsers;
}
```

The `activeUsers` computed signal calculates the filtered list only when `usersList` changes, not every time `activeUsers()` is read.

1.3 Avoid Unnecessary Effects

Effects (`effect()`) are for side effects – interacting with external systems (DOM, `localStorage`, network calls, logging). Avoid using effects for state transformations that only derive new state based on existing signals; use `computed()` for that. Misusing effects for state propagation can lead to unexpected change detection cycles or errors like `ExpressionChangedAfterItHasBeenChecked`.

Best Practice: Keep effect callbacks lightweight and focused on actual side effects. Perform internal state derivations using `computed()`.

2. Understanding the Performance Impact

Signals enable more granular tracking of state usage. This allows Angular to potentially optimize rendering updates more effectively than traditional Zone.js-based change detection, which often checks larger parts of the component tree. This forms the foundation for future performance enhancements, including zoneless applications[10][13].

Reduced Change Detection Scope: Angular can identify more precisely which components need checking when a signal changes.

More Predictable Data Flows: Signals often result in clearer state dependencies compared to complex RxJS chains for synchronous state management.

3. Optimizing Your Applications Using Signals

Practical strategies include:

- **Leverage Lazy Loading:** Load feature modules and their services/components on demand. Signals defined within these modules are only created when needed, optimizing initial load time and memory usage..
- **Use Computed Signals for Local Transformations:** Keep component-specific view model transformations local using computed() within the component, rather than exporting intermediate states from services.
- **Manage Effect Cleanup:** While signal dependencies are managed automatically, effects might create manual subscriptions (e.g., to RxJS observables), set timers (setInterval), or add event listeners. Use the onCleanup function provided within the effect callback to tear down these resources when the effect is destroyed or reruns, preventing memory leaks.

```
import { effect, signal, Injector, DestroyRef } from
'@angular/core';
import { interval, Subscription } from 'rxjs';

// Example within a component or service constructor/method with
injection context
constructor(private injector: Injector) {
  this.setupIntervalEffect();
}

setupIntervalEffect() {
  const counter = signal(0);

  effect((onCleanup) => {
    console.log(`Effect running. Counter: ${counter()}`); //
Depends on counter

    const timer = setInterval(() => {
      console.log('Timer tick inside effect');
      // Do something with the timer...
    }, 1000);

    // Register cleanup logic
    onCleanup(() => {
      console.log('Cleaning up interval timer...');
      clearInterval(timer);
    });
  }, { injector: this.injector }); // Pass injector if outside
constructor context

  // Example trigger:
  // setTimeout(() => counter.set(1), 5000); // Change signal to
trigger re-run & cleanup
}

// Alternative using DestroyRef (often simpler if effect is tied to
component/service lifecycle)
// constructor(private destroyRef: DestroyRef) {
//   const someSignal = signal(0);
//   effect(() => {
//     console.log(someSignal());
```

```
//     const sub: Subscription = interval(1000).subscribe(...);
//     // DestroyRef automatically calls cleanup when the context
(component/service) is destroyed
//     this.destroyRef.onDestroy(() => sub.unsubscribe());
//   });
// }
```

Advanced Use-Cases

1. Creating Reusable Signal Logic Across Components and Services

Encapsulate related state and logic within services that expose Signals. This promotes reusability and creates a single source of truth.

```
// flight-booking.facade.ts (Conceptual Example based on [33])
import { Injectable, signal, computed, inject } from
'@angular/core';
// Assume FlightService fetches data and Flight interface exists

@Injectable({ providedIn: 'root' })
export class FlightBookingFacade {
  // private flightService = inject(FlightService); // Service for
API calls

  // State Signals (private writable, public readonly/computed)
  private sourceFlights = signal<Flight[]>([]);
  private selectedFlightID = signal<number | null>(null);

  // Public computed signals for consumption by components
  readonly flights = this.sourceFlights.asReadonly();
  readonly selectedFlight = computed(() => {
    const id = this.selectedFlightID();
    const flights = this.sourceFlights();
    return id ? flights.find(f => f.id === id) ?? null : null;
  });
  readonly flightCount = computed(() =>
this.sourceFlights().length);

  // Methods to interact with the state (could involve async calls)
  async loadFlights(from: string, to: string): Promise<void> {
```

```
    // const loadedFlights = await
this.flightService.fetchFlights(from, to);
    // this.sourceFlights.set(loadedFlights);
    this.sourceFlights.set([ /* ...mock flights... */ ]); //
Example setter
    this.selectedFlightID.set(null); // Reset selection
  }

  selectFlight(id: number): void {
    this.selectedFlightID.set(id);
  }
}
```

Components inject `FlightBookingFacade` and use `flights()` or `selectedFlight()` without needing to know the internal implementation.

2. Using Signals in Complex Application Architectures (Signal Store Pattern)

For larger applications, a centralized store pattern can be beneficial. While dedicated libraries like NgRx Signal Store exist, you can implement a simpler version using a regular Angular service holding state signals.

- **Signal Store Service:** Holds root-level state Signals (e.g., `currentUser`, `cart`).
- **Feature Modules/Services:** Can inject the store, consume root state, and compute derived feature-specific state.
- **Components:** Inject relevant services and bind to the exposed Signals/computed Signals.

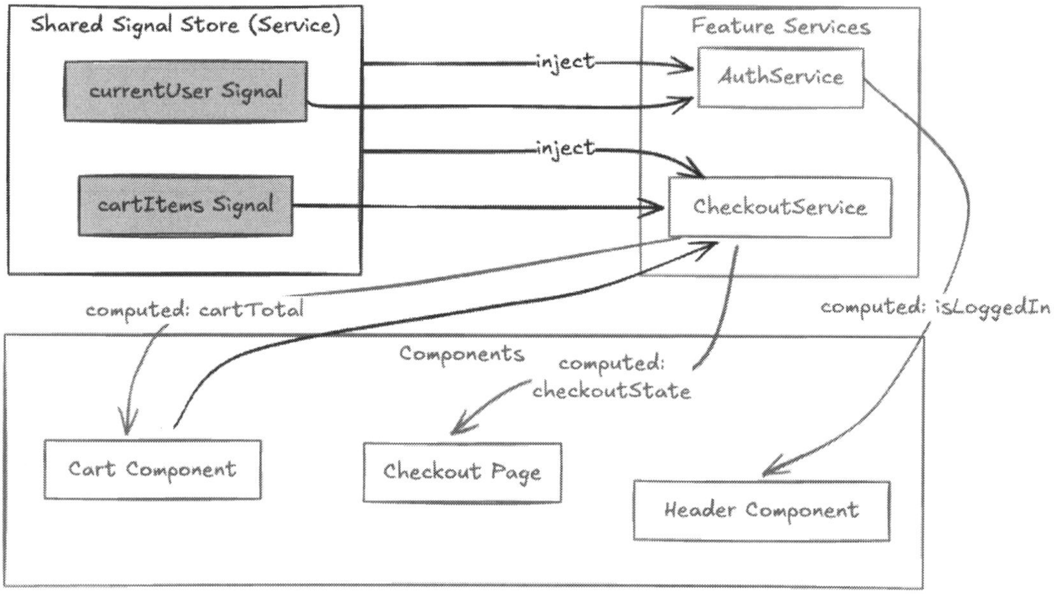

Figure 9.1 - A conceptual signal store flow

This promotes modularity, where the central store holds raw state, and features derive what they need.

3. Architectural Patterns for Signal-Based Applications

A layered architecture remains a robust pattern:

- **Data Services (Core):** Handle data fetching/persistence (e.g., HTTP calls). May use `resource()` or return Observables/Promises.
- **Business Logic/Domain Services (Facades/Stores):** Inject Data Services. Manage application state using Signals (`signal`, `computed`). Contain core business logic and expose state to the presentation layer. This is where patterns like the `FlightBookingFacade` or a simple Signal Store fit.
- **Presentation Layer (Components):** Inject Domain Services. Primarily bind to Signals for display. Delegate user actions to service methods. Keep component logic minimal and view-focused.

Common Errors and Troubleshooting

1. Debugging Angular Applications with Signals

- **Check Dependencies:** Ensure computed signals/effects read the intended source signals. Typos break reactivity.
- **Inspect Effects/Computeds:** Use `console.log` within computed functions (shows re-computation) or effects (shows execution and values). Use **browser dev tools** to inspect component properties.
- **Simplify:** Isolate issues by temporarily removing parts of computed chains or effect logic.

2. Common Issues

- **Forgotten Updates:** Remember to call `.set()` or `.update()` to change a `WritableSignal`. Variable reassignment doesn't work.
- **Circular Computed Signals:** Avoid `computedA` depending on `computedB` while `computedB` depends on `computedA`. This causes infinite loops. *Figure 9.2* shows what it looks like.
- **Effect Overuse:** Don't use `effect` for internal state derivation – use `computed`.
- **Writing in Computed/Effect:** By default, you cannot call `.set()`/`.update()` directly inside a computed or effect callback to prevent uncontrolled side effects and loops. Effects could allow writes via the `{ allowSignalWrites: true }` option per some earlier Angular versions, which has been removed now, but use this behaviour cautiously. Modifying state based on other state should primarily happen via computed for derivations or within component methods/service methods in response to events.

Figure 9.2 - Circular computed signals

3. Best Practices for Error Handling

- **Try/Catch in Computed Signals:** If a computation might fail (e.g., JSON parsing, accessing properties on potentially `null` values), wrap the risky logic in `try...catch` inside the `computed` function and return a sensible default or error indicator. Remember that errors thrown inside a `computed` are also memoized until a dependency changes.
- **Use Protective Checks:** Check for `null` or undefined signal values at the start of computed functions or effects if they depend on asynchronous or optional data.
- **Effect Error Boundaries:** Wrap side-effect logic (API calls, localStorage access) within effects using `try...catch` or status checks to handle failures gracefully and prevent application crashes.

Conclusion

This chapter explored the performance benefits Signals bring to Angular applications and how to fine-tune them for optimal results. We discussed advanced architectural patterns like using signals in services (Facades) or simple Signal Stores to structure applications effectively. We also covered common pitfalls like effect overuse, circular dependencies, and writing to signals improperly, along with strategies for troubleshooting and error handling.

Armed with this knowledge, you can build more efficient, maintainable, and scalable applications by leveraging Signals appropriately. Understanding these performance nuances and architectural considerations is key to mastering modern reactive development in Angular.

In the final chapter (Chapter 10), we will look at how Signals may shape the future of Angular and discuss new features and community trends on the horizon.

Chapter 10: The Future of Angular with Signals

Introduction

Over the past chapters, we explored how Signals fundamentally reshape state management and change detection in Angular. By introducing a more declarative and reactive approach, Signals pave the way for building clearer, more predictable, and higher-performing applications. We've journeyed from the basic building blocks (`signal`, `computed`, `effect`) through asynchronous operations, component integration (`input`, `output`, `model`), interoperability with RxJS, testing strategies, and advanced patterns.

Now, as Angular continues to evolve, it's essential to understand how Signals fit into the framework's longer-term trajectory. How might Signals continue to transform development practices, tooling, and the broader Angular ecosystem? This final chapter looks at the potential future, discussing the framework's direction, community trends, and possible enhancements around Signals in the coming years. We'll also provide guidance on how to stay current with these exciting developments.

Long-Term Implications

Signals represent more than just a new API; they indicate a shift in Angular's core philosophy towards more explicit reactivity and potentially improved performance.

1. Deeper Signal Integration

Angular's core team is progressively integrating Signals deeper into the framework. While we already have signal-based inputs, outputs, and two-way binding (model), we can anticipate further integration in areas like:

- **Router:** Future versions might leverage Signals for reactive route information (parameters, data) enabling more efficient updates triggered by route changes. Imagine accessing route params directly as a Signal.
- **Forms:** While integration is possible now, more streamlined, built-in Signal-based APIs for Angular Forms could offer finer-grained reactivity for form state, validity, and value changes, potentially simplifying complex validation scenarios.
- **HttpClient / Data Fetching:** Closer alignment between Angular's `HttpClient` and reactive primitives like Signals or resources could

emerge, perhaps offering utilities to directly create Signals or Resources from HTTP requests, simplifying async state management.
- **Zoneless Applications:** Signals are the key enabler for running Angular applications without Zone.js. Future development will likely focus on making zoneless the default or a much easier opt-in, relying on Signals to drive change detection.

2. Reducing Zone.js Reliance

Zone.js simplifies Angular by patching browser APIs to automatically trigger change detection. However, it adds overhead and can sometimes cause unexpected behavior. Signals provide a mechanism for Angular to know precisely when and where state has changed, reducing the need for Zone.js's broad monitoring. The ongoing effort towards "zoneless" Angular applications hinges on Signals as the primary driver for component updates. Achieving stable and widely adopted zoneless applications would represent a major performance and simplification milestone for the framework.

3. Smoother Migration Paths & Tooling

As Signals become more central, we can expect improved tooling, both official and community-driven, to ease the migration from older patterns (RxJS-heavy state management, `async` pipe usage for simple cases) to Signal-based approaches. This might include:

- More sophisticated schematics for automated refactoring.
- Specialized ESLint rules to guide developers towards idiomatic Signal usage.
- Enhanced debugging tools specifically for tracing Signal dependencies and updates.

Future Roadmap for the Angular Framework

Predicting the future is inherently speculative, but based on official communications (like blog posts, RFCs, roadmaps) and community discussions, we can anticipate the following directions. Please note that the version of Angular at the time of writing this book is **v20**. And the roadmap I'm sharing here is speculative and roadmaps can change.

(Speculative) Short-Term Future (Next 1-2 Major Versions)

- **Zoneless Improvements:** Continued refinements and potentially easier configuration for zoneless applications, making it a more viable option for new projects.

- **Documentation & Education:** Expanded official documentation, guides, and tutorials focusing on advanced Signal patterns and best practices, including zoneless scenarios.
- **Potential Signal Utilities:** Possible introduction of new utility functions within `@angular/core` or `@angular/core/rxjs-interop` to handle common reactive patterns or edge cases with Signals.

(Speculative) Mid-Term Future

- **Signal-Based Library APIs:** Core framework libraries like Forms and Router potentially offering primary APIs built around Signals for state tracking and reactivity.
- **Migration Tooling:** More mature official migration guides and automated tooling to assist large-scale transitions from RxJS or older patterns to Signals.
- **DevTools Enhancements:** Angular DevTools gaining deeper introspection capabilities specifically for visualizing Signal dependency graphs, tracking updates, and debugging reactive chains.

(Speculative) Long-Term Future

- **Zoneless by Default?:** A possible shift where zoneless becomes the default mode for new Angular applications, with Zone.js becoming optional for specific compatibility needs.
- **Core Re-architecture:** Potential deeper refactoring of Angular's internal rendering and change detection mechanisms to be fundamentally signal-driven.
- **Build-Time Optimizations:** Advanced static analysis of Signal usage during the build process to further optimize application performance and bundle size.

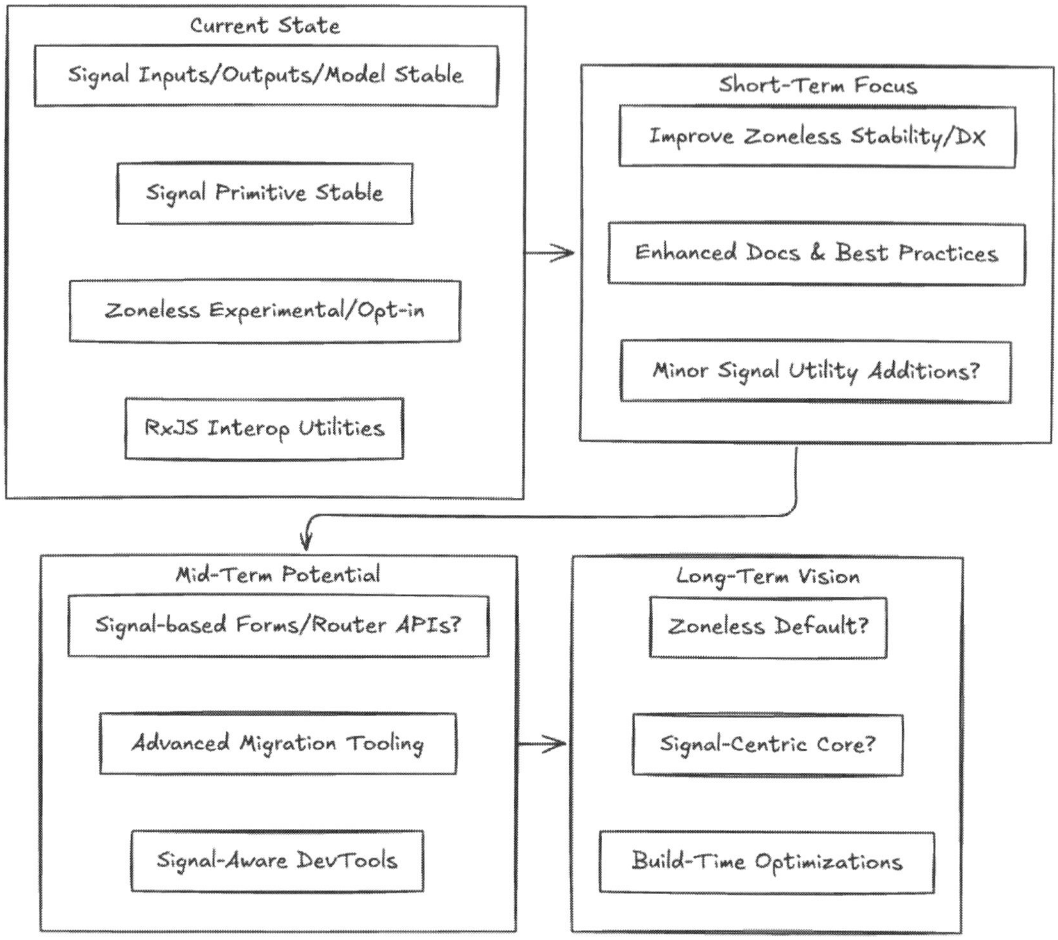

Figure 10.1 - Speculative Angular Signals Roadmap Stages

Community Trends

The Angular community is actively embracing Signals:

- **Signal-Based State Management:** Libraries like NgRx SignalStore and others are gaining traction, offering structured state management solutions built on top of Signals, providing alternatives to traditional NgRx or NGXS for certain use cases.
- **Custom Utilities & Libraries:** Expect to see more community-created utilities, directives, and libraries designed to work seamlessly with Signals, simplifying common patterns like form interactions or conditional rendering based on signal state.
- **Educational Resources:** Workshops, conference talks (ng-conf remains a key source), blog posts, and video tutorials focusing on Signals are proliferating, helping developers adopt best practices and understand

advanced concepts.

Future Developments

Looking ahead, several areas might see enhancements:

Enhancements and Features

- **Signal-Oriented CLI Generators:** Official Angular CLI schematics might evolve to generate boilerplate code (components, services) that defaults to using Signals for state management where appropriate.
- **Profiling and Debugging Tools:** Further integration into Angular DevTools to visualize Signal graphs, pinpoint unnecessary computations, and understand update propagation in real-time.
- **Server-Side Rendering (SSR):** Continued optimization of SSR and hydration strategies leveraging Signals, potentially precomputing signal values during SSR or optimizing the hydration process based on signal stability.

Speculations on Angular Evolution

- **Stronger Emphasis on 'Functional' Patterns:** Signals naturally align with functional programming concepts (pure computations for computed, managed side effects for effect), potentially encouraging more functional architectural patterns within the community.
- **Potential Deeper Integration with Web Platform:** As browser APIs evolve (e.g., around scheduling, concurrency, rendering), Angular might leverage these directly in conjunction with Signals for even more efficient updates and background processing.

Resources and Staying Current

The landscape is evolving rapidly. To keep up:

- **Official Angular Blog & Roadmap:** The primary source for release announcements, RFCs (Request for Comments), and roadmap updates.
- **Angular GitHub Repository:** Check issues and discussions for insights into ongoing development.
- **Angular DevTools:** Keep the browser extension updated; new versions often include enhanced debugging features.
- **Community Forums:** Participate in discussions on platforms like Discord, StackOverflow, and Reddit (r/Angular).
- **Conferences and Meetups:** Events like ng-conf, AngularConnect, and

local meetups often feature talks on the latest developments, including Signals.

- **Code with Ahsan (YouTube):** Of course, stay up to date with my YouTube channel
- **Ahsync Bytes (my blog):** In the fast-paced world, stay up to date with byte sized Angular updates, right in your mailbox.

Final Words

Signals represent a significant and exciting evolution in how Angular applications manage state and reactivity. They offer a path towards simpler code, reduced cognitive load, improved performance, and better alignment with modern reactive programming principles. This book has guided you from the fundamentals of Signals to advanced patterns, testing strategies, and now, a glimpse into their promising future.

Key Takeaways

- **Think Reactively:** Embrace the mindset of explicit state definition (`signal`) and derivation (`computed`) with managed side effects (`effect`).
- **Incremental Adoption:** Migrating to Signals doesn't have to be "all or nothing." Start where they provide the most benefit, leveraging interoperability with RxJS during the transition.
- **Stay Curious:** The Angular ecosystem is dynamic. Keep learning as new patterns, libraries, and best practices emerge around Signals.
- **Be Prepared for Future Updates:** The Angular team is actively refining and expanding Signal capabilities. Embrace these refinements to keep your applications modern and maintainable.

Encouragement for Continued Learning

As with any significant shift, the journey toward fully embracing Signals can be both exciting and challenging. Continue experimenting in your projects, contribute to community discussions, and share your insights and discoveries. The Angular ecosystem thrives on collaboration, and your experiences can help shape the future of Signals for everyone.

Conclusion

This completes our exploration of Signals in Angular, from the fundamental building blocks to advanced patterns, testing strategies, performance optimizations, and a forward-looking perspective on how Signals might continue to evolve. The Angular community and core team are highly active in refining the framework, and Signals are playing a pivotal role in that evolution.

Keep building, exploring, and sharing your experiences—your feedback and contributions help shape Angular's future. We hope this book has empowered you to leverage Signals confidently, and we encourage you to continue learning and stay connected with the vibrant Angular community as Signals continue to expand and mature.

Appendix

Glossary of Terms

Computed Signal

A read-only signal whose value is derived from one or more other signals. It automatically recalculates its value only when its dependencies change and caches the result.

Dependency Tracking

The core mechanism by which Angular automatically discovers which signals are read within a `computed` or `effect` function, creating a reactive graph to know what to update when a source signal changes.

Effect

A function that executes a side effect (like DOM manipulation, logging, or network calls) in response to changes in one or more signals. It is not used for deriving state.

Fine-Grained Reactivity

The ability of the framework to understand precisely which parts of the UI need to be updated when a piece

Printed in Poland
by Amazon Fulfillment
Poland Sp. z o.o., Wrocław

60312442R00096